About the Authors

Sebastian Hassinger

Sebastian Hassinger is an independent consultant and programmer who concentrates on all things Internet, with a special affinity for CGI programming and World Wide Web wackiness. Currently, clones of Sebastian work part-time at Apple Computer, Inc. and at OuterNet Connection Strategies. He's also occasionally sighted around his supposed home, in beautiful south Austin, Texas.

Sebastian is a graduate of Concordia University, Montreal, Canada, with a BA in English received in 1989. Before his tenure at Apple Computer, he worked for Simon Fraser University in Vancouver, BC, Canada, in the Macintosh Multimedia Laboratories (EXCITE) as a jack-of-all-programming-trades and disciplines. He contributed to the CGI programs in *HTML For Dummies*, was a co-author of *Foundations of WWW Programming*, and has written manuals and technical white papers for several high-tech products.

Sebastian Hassinger	Home: (512) 447-8764
2215 Post Road, Atp. 2012	Ofc: (512) 908-8517
Austin, TX 78704	FAX: (512) 206-0345
Internet e-mail: singe@outer.net	

Mike Erwin

Mike Erwin is an independent consultant and programmer who focuses primarily on Internet connectivity, CGI scripting, and large-scale operating systems development. Mike is a founding principal at OuterNet Connection Strategies, an Austin-based Internet Service Provider, that does network consulting for clients world-wide. Mike holds degrees in Computer and Information Science as well as Business Finance, and is currently engaged in managing much of the Internet offerings coming from Apple Computer, Inc.

Mike was a co-author of *Foundations of WWW Programming*, as well as on a smaller book about the Virtual Reality Modeling Language (VRML). He also contributed to the CGI programs in *HTML For Dummies*. In an earlier life, Mike wrote some short science fiction and fantasy works for gaming companies in the mid-1980s.

Mike Erwin	Home: (512) 302-0577
P.O. Box 26633	Ofc: (512) 345-3573
Austin, TX 78755-0633	FAX: (512) 908-8016
Internet e-mail: mikee@outer.net	Voice-Mail: (512) 908-8333

Acknowledgements

Sebastian Hassinger: This book would not exist without the patience, love, and understanding given me by Nina, Eyre, and Haefen. Thanks are due, too, to Gavin Bell, David Blair, and Tom Meyer for the help they gave me in collecting material for the book. Finally, a tip of the fedora to Ed Tittel, Mike Erwin, and Charlie Scott, my partners in crime.

Mike Erwin: I would like to personally extend my thanks to the other principals at OuterNet for letting me abuse their network and machinery for the experimentation so essential to writing this book. Many, many thanks to Thomas Caleshu, and Mark Meadows of the Arc VRML coding crew who answered my questions concerning how to set up a first-class VRML system.

This book is very much a team effort, so the thanks don't stop here. Together, both of us would like to thank Charlie Scott, of OuterNet Technologies, for his work on Chapters 1, 4, and 8, and for his many efforts on our behalf. We'd also like to thank Ed Tittel, for pulling this book together, for keeping us on track and on schedule, and for handling the interface with our publisher, IDG Books Worldwide.

Finally, we'd like to thank the whole IDG production team, including Ralph Moore, our project editor, Greg Emil, our cracker-jack technical editor, and Madame X, our wonderful manuscript editor, for all the help they gave in putting this book together. Last, but by no means least, we'd also like to thank our old friends and partners in adversity, Anne Marie Walker and Amy Pedersen, for giving us so many chances to work together.

The publisher would like to give special thanks to Patrick McGovern, without whom this book would not have been possible.

Mecklermedia's Official
Internet World™

60 Minute Guide to VRML

Sebastian Hassinger

and

Mike Erwin

IDG Books Worldwide, Inc.
Foster City, CA • Chicago, IL • Indianapolis, IN • Braintree, MA • Dallas, TX

Mecklermedia's Official Internet World™
60 Minute Guide to VRML
Published by

IDG Books Worldwide, Inc.
An International Data Group Company
919 East Hillsdale Boulevard, Suite 400
Foster City, CA 94404

Library of Congress Catalog Card No.:
ISBN 1-56884-710-6
Printed in the United States of America
First Printing, October 1995
10 9 8 7 6 5 4 3 2

Distributed in the United States by IDG Books Worldwide, Inc.

Published in the United States

ABOUT IDG BOOKS WORLDWIDE

VIII
WINNER
Eighth Annual
Computer Press
Awards ≥ 1992

IX
WINNER
Ninth Annual
Computer Press
Awards ≥ 1993

IDG
BOOKS
WORLDWIDE

Welcome to the world of IDG Books Worldwide.

IDG Books Worldwide, Inc. is a subsidiary of International Data Group, the world's largest publisher of computer-related information and the leading global provider of information services on information technology. IDG was founded more than 25 years ago and now employs more than 7,500 people worldwide. IDG publishes more than 235 computer publications in 67 countries (see listing below). More than fifty million people read one or more IDG publications each month.

Launched in 1990, IDG Books Worldwide is today the #1 publisher of best-selling computer books in the United States. We are proud to have received 3 awards from the Computer Press Association in recognition of editorial excellence, and our best-selling ...*For Dummies*™ series has more than 18 million copies in print with translations in 24 languages. IDG Books, through a recent joint venture with IDG's Hi-Tech Beijing, became the first U.S. publisher to publish a computer book in the People's Republic of China. In record time, IDG Books has become the first choice for millions of readers around the world who want to learn how to better manage their businesses.

Our mission is simple: Every IDG book is designed to bring extra value and skill-building instructions to the reader. Our books are written by experts who understand and care about our readers. The knowledge base of our editorial staff comes from years of experience in publishing, education, and journalism — experience which we use to produce books for the '90s. In short, we care about books, so we attract the best people. We devote special attention to details such as audience, interior design, use of icons, and illustrations. And because we use an efficient process of authoring, editing, and desktop publishing our books electronically, we can spend more time ensuring superior content and spend less time on the technicalities of making books.

You can count on our commitment to deliver high-quality books at competitive prices on topics consumers want to read about. At IDG, we value quality, and we have been delivering quality for more than 25 years. You'll find no better book on a subject than an IDG book

John J. Kilcullen

John Kilcullen
President and CEO
IDG Books Worldwide, Inc.

IDG Books Worldwide, Inc. is a subsidiary of International Data Group, the world's largest publisher of computer-related information and the leading global provider of information services on information technology. International Data Group publishes over 235 computer publications in 67 countries. More than fifty million people read one or more International Data Group publications each month. The officers are Patrick J. McGovern, Founder and Board Chairman; Kelly Conlin, President; Jim Casella, Chief Operating Officer. International Data Group's publications include: ARGENTINA'S Computerworld Argentina, Infoworld Argentina; AUSTRALIA'S Computerworld Australia, Computer Living, Australian PC World, Australian Macworld, Network World, Mobile Business Australia, Publish!, Reseller, IDG Sources; AUSTRIA'S Computerwelt Oesterreich, PC Test; BELGIUM'S Data News (CW); BOLIVIA'S Computerworld; BRAZIL'S Computerworld, Connections, Game Power, Mundo Unix, PC World, Publish, Super Game; BULGARIA'S Computerworld Bulgaria, PC & Mac World Bulgaria, Network World Bulgaria; CANADA'S CIO Canada, Computerworld Canada, InfoCanada, Network World Canada, Reseller; CHILE'S Computerworld Chile, Informatica; COLOMBIA'S Computerworld Colombia, PC World; COSTA RICA'S PC World; CZECH REPUBLIC'S Computerworld, Elektronika, PC World; DENMARK'S Communications World, Computerworld Danmark, Computerworld Focus, Macintosh Produktkatalog, Macworld Danmark, PC World Danmark, PC Produktguide, Tech World, Windows World; ECUADOR'S PC World Ecuador; EGYPT'S Computerworld (CW) Middle East, PC World Middle East; FINLAND'S MikroPC, Tietoviikko, Tietoverkko; FRANCE'S Distributique, GOLDEN MAC, InfoPC, Le Guide du Monde Informatique, Le Monde Informatique, Telecoms & Reseaux; GERMANY'S Computerwoche, Computerwoche Focus, Computerwoche Extra, Electronic Entertainment, Gamepro, Information Management, Macwelt, Netzwelt, PC Welt, Publish, Publish; GREECE'S Publish & Macworld; HONG KONG'S Computerworld Hong Kong, PC World Hong Kong; HUNGARY'S Computerworld SZT, PC World; INDIA'S Computers & Communications; INDONESIA'S Info Komputer; IRELAND'S ComputerScope; ISRAEL'S Beyond Windows, Computerworld Israel, Multimedia, PC World Israel; ITALY'S Computerworld Italia, Lotus Magazine, Macworld Italia, Networking Italia, PC Shopping Italy, PC World Italia; JAPAN'S Computerworld Today, Information Systems World, Macworld Japan, Nikkei Personal Computing, SunWorld Japan, Windows World; KENYA'S East African Computer News; KOREA'S Computerworld Korea, Macworld Korea, PC World Korea; LATIN AMERICA'S GamePro; MALAYSIA'S Computerworld Malaysia, PC World Malaysia; MEXICO'S Compu Edicion, Compu Manufactura, Computacion/Punto de Venta, Computerworld Mexico, MacWorld, Mundo Unix, PC World, Windows; THE NETHERLANDS' Computer! Totaal, Computable (CW), LAN Magazine, Lotus Magazine, MacWorld; NEW ZEALAND'S Computer Buyer, Computerworld New Zealand, Network World, New Zealand PC World; NIGERIA'S PC World Africa; NORWAY'S Computerworld Norge, Lotusworld Norge, Macworld Norge, Maxi Data, Networld, PC World Ekspress, PC World Nettverk, PC World Norge, PC World's Produktguide, Publish& Multimedia World, Student Data, Unix World, Windowsworld; PAKISTAN'S PC World Pakistan; PANAMA'S PC World Panama; PERU'S Computerworld Peru, PC World; PEOPLE'S REPUBLIC OF CHINA'S China Computerworld, China Infoworld, China PC Info Magazine, Computer Fan, PC World China, Electronics International, Electronics Today/Multimedia World, Electronic Product World, China Network World, Software World Magazine, Telecom Product World; PHILIPPINES' Computerworld Philippines, PC Digest (PCW); POLAND'S Computerworld Poland, Computerworld Special Report, Networld, PC World/Komputer, Sunworld; PORTUGAL'S Cerebro/PC World, Correio Informatico/Computerworld, MacIn; ROMANIA'S Computerworld, PC World, Telecom Romania; RUSSIA'S Computerworld-Moscow, Mir - PK (PCW), Sety (Networks); SINGAPORE'S Computerworld Southeast Asia, PC World Singapore; SLOVENIA'S Monitor Magazine; SOUTH AFRICA'S Computer Mail (CIO),Computing S.A.,Network World S.A., Software World; SPAIN'S Advanced Systems, Amiga World, Computerworld Espana, Communicaciones World, Macworld Espana, NeXTWORLD, Super Juegos Magazine (GamePro), PC World Espana, Publish; SWEDEN'S Attack, ComputerSweden, Corporate Computing, Macworld, Mikrodatorn, Natverk & Kommunikation, PC World, CAP & Design, Datalngenjoren, Maxi Data,Windows World; SWITZERLAND'S Computerworld Schweiz, Macworld Schweiz, PC Tip; TAIWAN'S Computerworld Taiwan, PC World Taiwan; THAILAND'S Thai Computerworld; TURKEY'S Computerworld Monitor, Macworld Turkiye, PC World Turkiye; UKRAINE'S Computerworld, Computers+Software Magazine; UNITED KINGDOM'S Computing /Computerworld, Connexion/Network World, Lotus Magazine, Macworld, Open Computing/Sunworld; UNITED STATES' Advanced Systems, AmigaWorld, Cable in the Classroom, CD Review, CIO, Computerworld, Computerworld Client/Server Journal, Digital Video, DOS World, Electronic Entertainment Magazine (E2), Federal Computer Week, Game Hits, GamePro, IDG Books, Infoworld, Laser Event, Macworld, Maximize, Multimedia World, Network World, PC Letter, PC World, Publish, SWATPro, Video Event; URUGUAY'S PC World Uruguay; VENEZUELA'S Computerworld Venezuela, PC World; VIETNAM'S PC World Vietnam.

For More Information...

For general information on IDG Books in the U.S., including information on discounts and premiums, contact IDG Books at 800-434-3422.

For information on where to purchase IDG's books outside the U.S., contact Christina Turner at 415-655-3022.

For information on translations, contact Marc Jeffrey Mikulich, Foreign Rights Manager, at IDG Books Worldwide; fax number: 415-655-3295.

For sales inquiries and special prices for bulk quantities, contact Tony Real at 800-434-3422 or 415-655-3048.

For information on using IDG's books in the classroom and ordering examination copies, contact Jim Kelly at 800-434-2086.

Internet World 60 Minute Guide to VRML is distributed in Canada by Macmillan of Canada, a Division of Canada Publishing Corporation; by Computer and Technical Books in Miami, Florida, for South America and the Caribbean; by Longman Singapore in Singapore, Malaysia, Thailand, and Korea; by Toppan Co. Ltd. in Japan; by Asia Computerworld in Hong Kong; by Woodslane Pty. Ltd. in Australia and New Zealand; and by Transworld Publishers Ltd. in the U.K. and Europe.

From Internet World Books

With INTERNET WORLD books, the first name in Internet magazine publishing and the first name in Internet book publishing now join together to bring you an exciting new series of easy-to-use handbooks and guides written and edited by the finest Internet writers working today.

Building upon the success of *Internet World* magazine and in close cooperation with its staff of writers, researchers, and Net practitioners, INTERNET WORLD books offer a full panoply of Net-oriented resources—from beginner guides to volumes targeted to business professionals, Internet publishers, corporate network administrators, and web site developers, as well as to professional researchers, librarians, and home Internet users at all levels.

These books are written with care and intelligence, with accuracy and authority, by the foremost experts in their fields. In addition, the bundling of potent connectivity and search software with selected titles in the series will broaden their inherent usefulness and provide immediate access to the vast fluid contents of the Internet itself.

One key element illuminates all of these features—their focus on the needs of the reader. Each book in this series is user-friendly, in the great tradition of IDG Books, and each is intended to bring the reader toward proficiency and authority in using the Internet to its fullest as a complement to all the other ways the reader creates, gathers, processes, and distributes information.

The scope of INTERNET WORLD books is to serve you as Internet user, whether you are a dedicated "nethead" or a novice sitting down to your first session on the Net. Whatever your level, INTERNET WORLD books are designed to fulfill your need. Beyond this, the series will evolve to meet the demands of an increasingly literate and sophisticated Net audience, presenting new and dynamic ways of using the Internet within the context of our business and personal lives.

Alan M. Meckler
Chairman and C.E.O.
Mecklermedia Corporation

Christopher J. Williams
Group Publisher and V.P.
IDG Books Worldwide, Inc.

Credits

IDG Books Worldwide, Inc.

Group Publisher and V. P.
Christopher J. Williams

Publishing Director
John Osborn

Senior Acquisitions Manager
Amorette Pedersen

Managing Editor
Kim Field

Editorial Director
Anne Marie Walker

Production Director
Beth A. Roberts

Project Editor
Ralph E. Moore

Manuscript Editor
Madame X

Technical Editor
Greg Emil

Composition and Layout
Benchmark Productions, Inc.

Proofreader
Adrienne Rebello

Indexer
Liz Cunningham

Book Design
Benchmark Productions, Inc.

Cover Design
Draper and Liew, Inc.

Mecklermedia Corporation

Senior Vice President
Tony Abbott

Managing Editor
Carol Davidson

Contents

Introduction

elcome to the "bleeding edge" of computer language technology! As we're writing this book, the Virtual Reality Modeling Language (VRML) remains a moving target. That's one reason why our book departs somewhat from IDG's normal format for its *60-Minute Guides*.

Whereas most of the *60-Minute Guides* focus exclusively on providing only those details necessary to learn and understand how to use a programming language, our coverage of VRML takes a more speculative look at where this language is going. It also provides a great many online resources to help you get current with the latest up-to-the-minute version of VRML, its tools and specification, and a number of interesting VRML sites to help you investigate and understand what the language can do.

About This Book

There are two approaches to using this book:

1. It is built as a series of three, 60-minute sections on VRML, each delivering a specific lesson or set of information on the subject.

2. It is meant to give an overview of the current state of VRML arts, and to provide signposts to current VRML information.

This book is not designed to be an exhaustive reference work on VRML. Rather, it is an introduction to VRML concepts and capabilities, and provides an entry point to the enormous collection of information, tools, and examples available on the Internet.

Section One: Introducing VRML

Chapters 1 through 3 cover the basics of VRML, including its motivation and design, its structure, syntax and concepts, and its advanced representational capabilities for describing three-dimensional spaces. By the time you finish this section, you will have a good idea about what VRML is, what it can do, and why it's an inevitable step toward the evolution of virtual reality modeling.

Section Two: Viewing VRML

Chapters 4 through 6 cover the VRML viewers currently available. It starts with X Windows and UNIX implementations, continues on to cover Macintosh implementations and future directions, and concludes with a discussion of the various versions available for Microsoft Windows (in its several distinct flavors). At the end of this section of the book, you should understand what's available on the various platforms and be able to appreciate their varying capabilities, maturity, strengths, and weaknesses.

Section Three: VRML Vistas

Chapters 7 through 10 take an in-depth look at three fascinating VRML sites and concludes with some ruminations on VRML's capabilities, limitations, and its future directions. This part of the book begins with a visit to a stunning post-modern experiment in hypermedia known as WAXweb. It then moves on to visit Virtual Vegas, an attempt to realize an entertainment-oriented gambling and arcade atmosphere on the Internet. Finally, we visit an architecturally-oriented virtual world, situated in the real world in the Variety Arts Center, in Los Angeles.

Each visit provides more than just a guided tour; it also discusses the design techniques and approaches its designers employed to build these sites. We discuss the problems the designers encountered, the implementation issues they faced, and the tools they built or used as workarounds. After a look at some implementations, we turn speculative and discuss VRML's potential, along with recommended applications, VRML's shortcomings, and future research and implementation directions. Throughout, we try to use concrete examples and to point to readily accessible Web sites wherever possible.

How to Use This Book

This book tells you what VRML is all about and how it works, including the language's keywords, syntax, and construction. Then it tells you what's involved in rendering and using VRML on a variety of platforms. After that, you'll explore some real-life examples in detail to get a flavor of what VRML can do, and how it can be used to build applications or virtual worlds.

When you type in any fragments of VRML code (or whole programs) be sure to copy the information exactly as you see it on the pages of this book. We've tested all the code to make sure it works properly and would like to save you the frustration of having to fix other people's mistakes.

We also recommend that you obtain the right set of VRML code libraries and an authoring tool before you try to start writing VRML code. While it is possible to build VRML programs by hand, it's a lot easier if you work within one of the authoring tools that are starting to appear on the marketplace. Wherever appropriate, we'll try to point out sources for such tools and to share our experiences in using them and in viewing their results.

Remember, too, that this book is intended as an overview of VRML and a discussion of its present capabilities and future potential. It is not a programming reference manual. Therefore, you'll find references to online sources for programming information in this book, but not a comprehensive programming manual, nor complete syntax diagrams, keyword lists, or other tools that you would expect from detailed training tools.

Where to Go from Here

Like all the *60-Minute Guides*, each part of this book on VRML builds on what comes before it. Therefore, we strongly recommend that you set aside about three hours, and spend one of those hours on each of the three parts of this book. It'll make a great deal more sense if you read all three parts in order.

Once you've made an initial pass through the materials, we also expect that you'll find the online resources particularly useful. That's why we've built the Appendix as a chapter-by-chapter listing of all the URLs in the book. To help you deal with any specialized terms we use, you'll also find a comprehensive Glossary. It should help you figure out what words like "scene" and "node" mean within VRML's particular definitions of those terms. You'll not only find yourself revisiting a nice chunk of computer graphics terminology, you'll probably even expand your vocabulary along the way—at least we did!

Section

One

Introducing VRML

*t*his part of the book includes Chapters 1 through 3 and covers the basics of VRML, including its motivation and design, its structure, syntax and concepts, and its advanced representational capabilities for describing three-dimensional spaces. By the time you finish this section, you should have a good idea about what VRML is, what it can do, and why it's an inevitable step in the evolution of virtual reality modeling.

In Chapter 1, "The Motivation for VRML," you'll cover the basics of VRML and its guiding implementation and design principles. Here, you'll learn that VRML is a generic text-based language that describes how to construct 3-D images on-the-fly. You'll also learn the basic vocabulary and concepts for 3-D modeling and graphics displays.

In Chapter 2, "Inside VRML: Structure, Syntax, and Concepts," you'll be formally introduced to the language. Here, you'll learn about VRML's basic characteristics, its object orientation, and the various types and attributes supplied in its built-in object definitions. You'll also come to appreciate VRML's control structures, its operators and syntax, and how the language is put together to build programs.

Finally, in Chapter 3, "Advanced VRML: The Saga Continues," you'll encounter the language's more sophisticated side. You'll learn about its shape nodes, property nodes, and how graphical objects can be rotated and transformed to match apparent changes in light sources, orientation, and points of view. Some of VRML's most interesting capabilities are covered in the concluding sections of this chapter—namely, its ability to map surface textures and patterns onto the many surfaces the language can describe and control, and its ability to explicitly handle multiple light sources and viewpoints (called cameras).

By the end of Section One, you'll have a good idea of what the VRML language looks like, how it represents three-dimensional objects, and how it handles perspective and viewing information. With all this information under your belt, you'll also have an appreciation for what VRML can do and how it does it!

## CHAPTER 1

The Motivation for VRML

Introduction

*t*oday, there's surge of activity to make the Internet and particularly the World Wide Web (WWW, or the Web) easier and more productive to use. Virtual Reality Modeling Language (VRML) is the most promising of a variety of three-dimensional modeling alternatives, providing a compact grammar that allows Web users to navigate and interact with realistic looking places and spaces. VRML is a generic text-based language that describes how to construct 3-D images on-the-fly. In this book, we'll explore this exciting new language and uncover some of its mysteries.

In our study of VRML's capabilities and in our tests of various applications that rely on this emerging technology, we have concluded that the VRML specification could possibly represent the Internet's next big step in interface design. In much the same way that the delivery of a common, powerful hypertext language—namely, HTML (HyperText Markup Language)—led to the explosion of the Web, in the near future we expect a paradigm shift to an online world.

This world will be filled with fully rendered 3-D offices, storefronts, and conference areas. No more *point and click* with the mouse. Rather, it will be *grab and twist* or *pull and manipulate* with a gloved-hand. And instead of your limited view on a flat screen monitor, you'll be using a set of goggles, or some other, more panoramic viewing device. This new paradigm should result in a more human-oriented interface, scoped in real-space, and rendered completely on-the-fly.

From the VRML Specification 1.0 Document

The Virtual Reality Modeling Language (VRML) is a language for describing multi-participant interactive simulations—virtual worlds networked via the global Internet and hyperlinked with the World Wide Web. All aspects of virtual world display, interaction and internetworking can be specified using VRML. It is the intention of its designers that VRML become the standard language for interactive simulation within the World Wide Web.

The first version of VRML allows for the creation of virtual worlds with limited interactive behavior. These worlds can contain objects which have hyperlinks to other worlds, HTML documents or other valid MIME types. When the user selects an object with a hyperlink, the appropriate MIME viewer is launched. When the user selects a link to a VRML document from within a correctly configured WWW browser, a VRML viewer is launched. Thus VRML viewers are the perfect companion applications to standard WWW browsers for navigating and visualizing the Web. Future versions of VRML will allow for richer behaviors, including animations, motion physics and real-time multi-user interaction.

The full text of this document can be found at the following URL:

```
http://vrml.wired.com/vrml.tech/vrml10-3.html
```

From its very inception, VRML's developers intended it to be a separate but parallel markup language, similar to HTML, but a distinct and different language, nonetheless. VRML is not meant to augment HTML, nor even to be an extension to HTML. HTML supplies a common text delivery mechanism for the Web, whereas VRML is meant to handle all forms of graphic and visual presentation. Just as a Web page is comprised of different elements of different classes, such as 2-D images, sounds, and formatted text, a VRML document (or *scene*, as it is normally called) represents a 3-D backdrop against which humans can interact with information. Following this approach, polygonal objects would be coded in VRML, and rendered when a user retrieves a scene across the network, in much the same way that HTML is rendered to display a 2-D text and graphical image.

VRML also supports a hyperlinking feature that resembles the Uniform Resource Locator (URL) system used on the Web today. By selecting hyperlinked objects, VRML browsers can transport users to another site, with other images and scenes constructed as they arrive. In fact, VRML's not-too-distant future should have a wealth of enhancements in store. While real-time interaction is probably the biggest change involved, we can easily predict the development of a system of gateways—comparable to the Web's Common Gateway Interface (CGI)—that allows different scenes to be erected every time a page is retrieved, making each visit a unique and rewarding experience.

We must point out that in order to see VRML objects, you need a viewer that supports the language. Consider this example: you connect to the *outer.net* Web site, and select a scene that contains a VRML walk-through for a new office building that the site's owners plan to build next year. Since VRML documents (like HTML documents) are text-based and rendered on-the-fly, you would be able to download the scene to your browser, but would need a helper application to view the three-dimensional scene. Without a helper application, a VRML document would appear as a long, obtuse collection of text elements. The exchange of information between the Web browser and the proper helper application is handled by a set of MIME definitions that select and launch the right VRML viewer application. This, in a nutshell, is how VRML can extend today's two-dimensional Web into three-dimensional space. (MIME stands for Multimedia Internet Mail Extensions, a specification for handling multipart and multitype mail messages.)

In this book, we'll take a look at several different VRML viewers. Today, there are only a few available because VRML technology is at the beginning of its development curve. However, we expect this technology to grow rapidly and the tools and software offerings to increase in variety, capability, and scope.

Our primary focus is to familiarize you with VRML basics, and to give you concrete examples about how to use this language to create scenes of your own. We'll also discuss some future offerings you might expect from the developers of VRML viewer applications. Finally, we'll explore some of VRML's potential uses that will soon be sprouting up in almost every field. We'll begin our explorations with a quick look at the foundations of visual modeling and its prior uses in the computing field.

Background of 3-D Imaging and Modeling

For nearly twenty years, Computer Aided Design (CAD) software has allowed engineers and architects to create 3-D representations of objects. CAD systems let their users view the end result of a designer's work before a product is actually fabricated. Many earlier CAD systems were limited to wireframe drawings, which offered neither perspective, textures, color, nor lighting effects. Today, this has been enhanced by the incorporation of ray-tracing and rendering software into CAD systems; these "special effects" support multiple points of view on designs; control virtual light sources; and include light and texture filters, along with a variety of other visual effects intended to help humans "see" renderings of CAD designs in ever more realistic ways.

Such wireframe diagrams and their more sophisticated successors have traditionally been used for engineering applications. When it comes to looking at a valve or a machine part, the need for realistic, virtual presentation was not a primary goal driving the rendering and visualization efforts involved. But the stellar advancements in microcomputer technology have provided considerable impetus for an easily controlled, fully rendered 3-D system that can present a virtual interactive world, rather than just the design specs for a machine part. The rise of microcomputer applications, such as *Strata Studio Pro* and *RenderMan*—both of which can be used to create entire virtual movies with fully rendered object primitives—argues that a marriage of the global Internet with such ability is not only irresistible, but immanent.

Current System Limitations

There's been a lot of discussion lately about how the Internet has finally become accessible to ordinary people. Inevitably, the standardized Internet signposting system, known as the World Wide Web, has been the centerpiece for such discussions. In fact, the Web introduced a standard syntax for referring to and accessing Internet hosts—called a Uniform Resource Locator (URL) based on a standardized Uniform Resource Name (URN) scheme—and left this standard open for extensions and enhancements. This open architecture permits the introduction of other Internet applications, one of which is three-dimensional rendering.

Locating Resources Uniformly

A URL supplies a standard nomenclature for addressing Internet services using Web browsers. For example, a file transfer protocol (FTP) service could be accessed at:

```
ftp://ftp.cdrom.com
```

a *gopher* service at:

```
gopher://gopher.ibm.com
```

and an HTML language service at:

```
http://www.outer.net
```

We'll get to VRML URLs later.

Many of the services available via the World Wide Web are based on TCP/IP networking services made available long before the advent of graphical user interfaces. For example, FTP provides a means for file exchange over the Internet. You can use a variety of Web browsers or other client applications to retrieve files from an Internet host. These applications provide a transparent umbrella over the directory structure on the host machine's native file system but unless you know exactly where you're going and what you're looking for, it can be difficult to navigate.

Gopher servers, like FTP servers, are used primarily to browse and transfer files. But instead of supplying a straightforward view of a host machine's directory structure, as FTP does, Gopher allows you to associate text on a menu with a file's location or another server entirely! So, instead of a file named "aus950720.jpg" you would see a menu entry like "Cloud-Cover Map of Austin, Texas—July 20, 1995". Clicking this text with your mouse causes the automatic transfer of the file to your system. This approach adds descriptive content to a simple file label, and helps account for Gopher's continuing popularity in the Internet community.

Several limitations make FTP and Gopher services unappealing for information retrieval. As with most personal software packages, many information service providers would like to offer WYSIWYG (What You See Is What You Get) capabilities. With FTP and Gopher, you can't see anything until you've waited for the download to complete. In other words, these services aren't real-time, nor do they offer the ability to browse materials before making them local.

Imagine that instead of downloading the Austin weather JPEG image file, and then launching an image viewer, you could click on the "Cloud-Cover Map of Austin, Texas—July 20, 1995" text and have the image appear before your eyes. You can, in fact, make this very thing happen today. But if you wanted to look at a weather history for Austin on July 20 over the past decade, in the form of a document consisting of pre-formatted text with multiple fonts, with bold and italicized headings, and tables containing the historical data, you'd have to know at least two things:

1. That such a document did indeed exist (or an application to build such a document on-the-fly was available for use).
2. The name and location of this document, so that you could retrieve it on demand.

Given these two items of information, you could download the document using Gopher or FTP. But now, format issues rear their ugly heads. If we assume the document is stored in Microsoft Word 6.0c for Windows format, you'd have to pray that your copy of Microsoft Word 5.1a for Macintosh would convert it correctly. The platform dependencies and format handling issues for this kind of approach are obvious and painful.

Now imagine that this document is platform independent, that it uses a simple text-coding system to produce the desired effects, and that it can include JPEG weather maps in-line. What's more, it can immediately be retrieved from the Internet and viewed on-the-fly with an inexpensive (or free!) browser that understands the built-in coding. What you've imagined is a fast, standard, and powerful way to present information.

In fact, HTML already provides a standard way to present such information on the Internet. HTML's look-and-feel has become nearly synonymous with the World Wide Web, and it is definitely the most recognizable and easy-to-use Internet service. Within HTML, hypertext is highlighted; by selecting such text with your mouse, you can link to another portion on an HTML page, another page on the same host, an HTML page on another host, or a different service altogether (e.g., FTP, Gopher, VRML).

Browsing for Browsers?

There are lots of Web browsers available that can render HTML documents on a variety of platforms. The two most popular are Mosaic and Netscape, both with versions for MS Windows, Macintosh, and X Windows, downloadable from these respective FTP locations:

```
ftp://ftp.ncsa.uiuc.edu

ftp://ftp.mcom.com
```

Netscape comes highly recommended because it can interface easily with some of the VRML browsers described later in this book, including WebSpace.

A Movement from HTML

A series of linked HTML documents almost seems alive. It's dynamic, flows freely, and may have clickable image maps, allowing you to select a link from a 2-D graphical representation of an object or scene. Some HTML documents even change on their own, constantly updating themselves with new data or links with the help of an underlying program or script.

Life, however, isn't lived in only two dimensions—objects and environments have width, breadth, height, shadows, textures, and perspective, accentuated by a plenitude of other sensory information. By denying ourselves these other sensory inputs, we deny ourselves a large amount of available information. (For an amusing venture into this philosophy from the perspective of a 2-D square, read Edward Abbott Abbott's *Flatland*.)

Let's revisit an imaginary version of the HTML weather document we talked about earlier. We'd get the same document as before, but now our JPEG map is a clickable hyperlink to a VRML document. When we click the map, we'd get an image of the cloud cover over Austin, with the topology and large buildings shown in 3-D. We're now able to rotate the image, allowing us to view it from nearly any angle. Instead of white streaks painted over a flat green background and an outline of the city showing only the cloud cover, we're able to see how high the clouds are and their actual thicknesses. Clicking on a specific cloud delivers an HTML document with information about what type of cloud it is and its general properties. Add a third dimension, and information that was unavailable to us from a 2-D JPEG is now visible and available.

In its current form, it would be difficult for HTML to create and send 3-D images like the ones we've just described. If you did this kind of thing with HTML, the server would have to generate an image at your request and send it to your browser in JPEG or some other format, whereupon you could render and view it. If you wanted to change perspective, you'd have to send this new viewpoint information back to the server. It would then perform the necessary calculations, generate a new image, and send it back to you.

While this approach is doable, it wouldn't be very efficient. Transmission times could become even more unbearable than they currently are. 3-D image modeling could easily cripple a server, especially if it received numerous requests for such service, as so many HTML servers do. A possible alternative might be to pre-generate multiple images from various perspectives, and then store them on the server, ready for shipment over the wire at the browser's request. Even so, transmission time lags would still apply, and the change to a new perspective would be jerky and not match user requirements. In other words, time delays and jerky transitions could destroy any hint of realistic perspective shifts.

Virtual reality, like artificial intelligence, is one of the Holy Grails of computer science. We may never know if either of these goals is attained, because interested parties will keep arguing about exactly what these goals are for the foreseeable future. Whether an object is virtually "real" or not depends almost entirely on your own perspective.

There are many researchers who work in virtual reality who say, "Why would I want to make something seem real, anyway? That would be boring." They're not saying VR should only be used for psychedelic experiences—what we think they mean is: "Why not make VR more amenable to human cognition?" Instead of walking into a virtual library and looking at the spines of books for their titles, why not make each virtual book itself *reflect* the information it contains. For example, information on fish might be accessed by touching (or clicking on) a 3-D image of a fish. Specifically, clicking on the fish's eye might supply information about the visual acuity of fish, or about the anatomical structures of a fisheye. Following this approach, the information *becomes* the object, and the object the information.

Virtual reality, with the wealth of information it can provide and the channels of communication it opens, is where 3-D modeling and the World Wide Web can effectively meet.

History and Foundations of VRML

VRML was first developed as a specification to organize the reality modeling work underway at different organizations into a single unified programming language. Not surprisingly, VRML discussions began in 1994 at the first WWW conference in Geneva, where a plan for its initial implementation originated.

Several of the attendees at this meeting were already involved with projects to deliver 3-D graphical visualization tools that could interoperate with the Internet and the WWW. These attendees agreed on the need for a common language, so that a "scene description" could be transmitted to almost anyone, anywhere.

Basically, what this group described was analogous to the HTML system, except that it dealt with 3-D visual interactions, rather than with static text and graphic pages. The project was quickly termed *VRML*, which at the time stood for Virtual Reality Markup Language, but the word *Markup* was soon changed to *Modeling* to better reflect the nature of the project's goals.

Directly after the Geneva conference, the *www-vrml* mailing list was created to discuss the salient aspects of the emerging 1.0 version of VRML. Mark Pesce, the group's moderator, drove these early stages by drafting the first VRML requirements document. Now the search was underway for an open and extensible technology that could easily be adapted to VRML.

Many options were presented and discussed by the mailing list's members, but after much deliberation, the Open Inventor File format (OIF) created by Silicon Graphics, Inc. (SGI), emerged as the most obvious choice. The OIF format was ASCII–based, which was a primary requirement in keeping with HTML. OIF also supported all of the graphical elements and operations that the initial VRML requirements document specified: everything from lighting effects to ambient properties were included.

In fact, a subset of OIF, combined with some necessary networking properties, formed the basis for VRML. Gavin Bell of SGI, in collaboration with mailing list contributors, developed the original file format into a VRML–specific format that helped launch the project.

The VRML Contenders

In the sections that follow, we'll provide you with brief overviews of some of the main contenders that vied to become VRML, starting with the winner—Open Inventor from SGI.

Open Inventor

Open Inventor, an object-oriented 3-D toolkit created by SGI, offers a robust set of graphical elements for the creation of interactive views. Open Inventor is distributed as a set of programming libraries and includes a whole variety of 3-D primitives for use in graphics programming. Objects like cubes, polygons, text, materials, cameras, lights, trackballs, and handle boxes can all be controlled using the Inventor libraries. It is a well defined, comprehensive set of applications and libraries that can speed up the development of interactive graphics applications.

Although the Inventor file format was used to create the VRML specification, Inventor itself is far more than just an interactive graphic file format; it is a complete rendering toolkit with everything you need to create a 3-D application. Open Inventor, built on top of OpenGL, supports animation, PostScript printing, and 3-D interaction, as well as allowing its users to create new objects based on the ones it provides as primitives.

One of the reasons for the creation of VRML is that like most of its brethren, Open Inventor is both hardware- and software-specific, making it difficult to create the kinds of cross-platform, cross-application, and cross-network uses that Internet users expect.

More information about Silicon Graphics' Open Inventor toolkit can be found at the following URL:

```
http://www.sgi.com/Technology/Inventor.html
```

Web OOGL

The *Object-Oriented Graphics Language for the World Wide Web*, or *Web OOGL*, has the distinction of being a tried-and-true method for representing 3-D information through a textual file format. Developed at the Geometry Center at the University of Minnesota several years ago, its primary application is as a geometric visualization format for physics, mathematics, and engineering. Web OOGL's simple syntax includes many of the things that eventually showed up in VRML, including a hierarchical structure, color control, textures, and polygons with shared vertices. You can view OOGL's specification at:

```
http://www.geom.umn.edu/software/geomview/docs/ooglman.html
```

Web OOGL is a non-proprietary format, and a free browser is available at the Geometry Center. Called *Geomview*, this browser is easy to extend, so that it may support a variety of prototyped Web OOGL features. One of the more interesting features proposed is the ability to grab not just local OOGL files, but entire URLs to OOGL files. With this ability, the bits and pieces of a VRML world could be brought in from anywhere on the Internet!

For more information on Geomview, please consult this URL:

```
http://www.geom.umn.edu/software/geomview/docs/geomview_toc.html
```

Autodesk's Cyberspace Description Format

The *Cyberspace Description Format (CDF)*, is a highly detailed VRML proposal from Autodesk that's based on their *Cyberspace Development Kit.* It's structurally similar to VRML, but already contains many more extensions. Like VRML, CDF strives to be declarative rather than procedural: It's essentially a description of a 3-D world, not an algorithm to create one. CDF's other goals include platform independence, small size to require little bandwidth, a concise syntax, object-orientation (though not to any particular language model), and expandability. An impressive description of the CDF specification can be found at:

```
http://vrml.wired.com/proposals/cdf/cdf.html
```

Another interesting feature that CDF incorporates is the ability to delegate parsing various file formats, such as 3-D Studio, Open Inventor, DXF, OOGL, and others. When a CDF parser encounters such a file, it may not be able to parse it, but it can call a "helper parser" that can either create the necessary objects, or rewrite the file in CDF format, so that the CDF parser can understand it.

A File Format for the Interchange of Virtual Worlds

A File Format For the Interchange of Virtual Worlds (its only title, which we'll abbreviate here as AFF) was proposed by Bernie Roehl and Kerry Bonin in May 1994. AFF is quite similar to the existing VRML specifications, though it was never fully fleshed out.

AFF is exactly what its title represents—a file format consisting of tags with specific properties that compose a 3-D virtual world (e.g., a material, a shape, or a texture map). The main argument behind this proposal is that such files should be comprised of ASCII text. This makes the files human-readable, platform-independent, and transmittable using a variety of means: from e-mail, to network delivery, to applications via TCP/IP sockets.

A draft of the AFF proposal can be found at:

    http://vrml.wired.com/proposals/ffivw.html

Multitasking Extensible Messaging Environment (Meme)

Meme, an interactive development package from Immersive Systems, Inc., allows programmers to create virtual worlds and act within them. Today, Meme's main drawback is that it runs only on DOS systems with 80386 processors or better.

Meme does, however, incorporate a modeling language similar to VRML, in which programmers write "modules" to create virtual worlds. Modules may be created and loaded at any time while you are in a particular virtual world. Borrowing terminology from William Gibson's sci-fi stories, each user also runs a "cyberspace deck module" that supplies code for all recognized I/O devices (such as data gloves or mice) and for interacting with the virtual environment.

Immersive Systems has made an overview of Meme available on the World Wide Web at:

    http://remarque.berkeley.edu/~marc/overview.html

Labyrinthe-VRML Specification Version 1.3.1

Labyrinthe and its VRML working specification are early versions of what was to become VRML itself. It was created by the Labryrinthe

Group, made up of Anthony Parisi (*dagobert@netcom.com*) and Mark Pesce (*mpesce@netcom.com*), two of the original VRML pioneers.

Labyrinthe is a parsing algorithm for VRML world files that supplies the engine for a VRML world browser. It's quite a straightforward language. A VRML world file is made up of scenes; scenes are made up of objects; and objects are made up of polygonals and qualities (material, color, and texture). This hierarchy of worlds, scenes, and objects gives you a taste of what VRML is like, and provides interesting insights into how a standard is made.

The 1.3.1 working specification of Labyrinthe-VRML can be found at:

```
http://vrml.wired.com/proposals/labspec.html
```

Manchester Scene Description Language

Developed at the University of Manchester, the *Manchester Scene Description Language (MSDL)* was developed to help combat redundancy and increase portability between graphics developers' applications. It closely resembles VRML and has the advantage of being in real-world use at the University of Manchester. MSDL was originally coded for UNIX systems (Sun and HP-UX), but has also been ported to DOS. It can be retrieved from:

```
ftp://ftp.mcc.ac.uk/pub/cgu/MSDL
```

These precursors to VRML helped to define the kinds of functionality and syntax that would eventually be incorporated into the "official" language itself. They are worth investigating further, especially if you're interested in learning about alternate approaches to VR modeling.

What Can You Do with VRML?

Architecture

One likely area where VRML will be integrated and deployed is real estate design and modeling. Several applications already exist to allow potential purchasers to erect and tear down multitudes of variations on proposed structure—without ever laying a single foundation.

By using such applications, builders have a clearer picture of the design and construction requirements before they start building. Such variables as winter versus summer sunlight, land grades, toilet piping, and wallpaper choices can be adjusted quickly and easily to suit designers' or buyers' needs. VRML can build on these already powerful systems by networking all of the parties involved, even if they are halfway across the planet.

Online Conferencing

Another exciting application that is very close to deployment is the Online Conference Room. Consider a private company with offices all over the world. Using VRML to create a shared but virtual meeting space, the company can meet to extend its corporate strategy or deliver next year's financial projections, without participants ever leaving their offices.

Currently, many national and international telecommunications companies plan to use VRML to define "virtual phone booths." Some are even considering creating ties between such virtual environments and their voice networks to support on-the-fly conferencing between any number of customers at any locations they service. While this may still be a remote possibility, this approach may make it possible to use public networks for group encounters in virtual reality anytime, anyplace (at least where there's an appropriate connection).

Virtual Storefronts

One of the most exciting scenarios where VRML should naturally excel is in the online rendering of goods and services. When the VRML standard becomes fully integrated with browser technology, we can expect to see such things as a 20- or 200-floor department store on the Net, stocked to the brim with the latest fashion selections.

Of course real opportunities for virtual shopping also rely on significant advancements in Web security and online shopping systems. These are being explored as we speak, but the inherent problems are by no means solved, nor have widely accepted standards for commerce and shopping yet emerged.

The first Virtual Stores we see will probably be owned by computer vendors, offering software that can be delivered on the spot or services that can be performed anywhere. However, we still have a couple of years to wait before Virtual WalMart comes to our electronic neighborhoods.

Scientific and Medical Research

Two areas where VRML should prove most useful are in science and medicine. Several universities and organizations have already begun to exploit its uses in these realms. Virginia Tech University, for example, has created 3-D models of atomic orbitals; Oxford University lets you build your own cell membranes; and NCSA has already defined astronomical objects like black holes, galaxies, and other cosmological elements in VRML format.

Someday VRML will provide tools to define learning environments for students that will allow them to completely visualize objects they couldn't otherwise see or interact with. Logical choices could include a 3-D human brain map or even a completely dissectable virtual human body!

Entertainment

The entertainment aspects of virtual reality and VRML seem limitless and will probably become the most exploited avenue for this technology. Interactive movies or virtual reality mystery games are obvious candidates for VRML entertainment. However, technological limitations in delivering full-blown virtual realities may keep most games at the building-block geometric level of Tetris for quite awhile.

Many online entertainment sites offer a taste of what's to come. Virtual Vegas (a site you'll explore in Chapter 8) offers a 3-D virtual gambling world where you can interact with the environment and watch movies. Another lets you explore a 3-D fractal; while a third takes you through an interactive origami lesson. No more wasting paper learning how to fold!

For the 3-D fractals, visit Leemon Baird's home page at:

```
http://kirk.usafa.af.mil:80/~baird/vrml/
```

For an interactive origami lesson, point your browser at the following URL:

```
http://www.neuro.sfc.keio.ac.jp/~aly/polygon/vrml/ika/
```

Introduction to VRML Terms

VRML was designed to use the ASCII character set for a variety of reasons. One reason is to permit it to be human-readable and easily written with a variety of tools. ASCII format means that no special processing is required and it assures platform independence, an absolute must for a networking language.

Performance was another consideration driving VRML's design. As we mentioned earlier, it could be terribly time consuming if rendering an object took place on a server with the image sent to the requesting system. Instead, a VRML server sends a VRML document, which is then translated and rendered by a VRML–capable browser on the requesting machine. This saves significant amounts of time and makes transformations and perspective shifts much smoother.

The VRML language itself is essentially a way to create objects, where each object defines a *tool* that can be used to help create a 3-D virtual world. These objects are called *nodes*. A node may be a specific geometric shape (e.g., a sphere or a cube), a texture, or even a movement. Each node has characteristics, or *fields*, that set it apart from other nodes; for example, its size, the image it uses for a texture, or its angle of rotation.

A node can also be given a unique *name* so that you may call it somewhere else in a virtual world. This greatly increases the flexibility of your objects. Some nodes are allowed to have *child* nodes, which means that they can contain other nodes. A node that has a child is called a *group* node, with the potential to be a very elaborate object. Further details on how the language works will be covered in the next chapter. For now, it suffices to say that VRML supports a rich and varied representational structure.

Summary

In this chapter we've provided an overview of VRML's creation, its intended purposes, and some ideas about what you can expect by way of interactive graphic developments over the next several years. We also briefly explored how VRML is structured, and discussed the possibilities inherent in using VRML on the WWW. We hope that you are as excited as we are about bringing this new language to the forefront, because we believe it could be used to create a more dynamic, productive global Internet.

In the next chapter, we'll peel back the veneer, and see what's going on inside the language, as we begin our exploration of VRML's capabilities and syntax.

## CHAPTER 2

Inside VRML

Structure, Syntax, and Concepts

The First Step Is a Doozy!

*t*he Virtual Reality Modeling Language has only recently achieved a relative degree of stability. The first formal VRML specification was released to the public on November 2, 1994. As of this writing, it is in its third draft, dated May 26, and substantial development efforts based on this specification are currently underway.

VRML occupies a peculiar place in the spectrum of programming languages, midway between a general-purpose language like C++, Lisp, or Perl and a page description formatting language like PostScript, troff, or HTML. This stems from the fact that although VRML has a very specific purpose—describing three-dimensional scenes and objects—this task is so complex that the language needs many of the features of a more generalized programming language. While this can make the initial learning curve relatively steep, VRML's complexity ensures that not only is it capable of bringing the third dimension to the Web, it also leaves room for growth.

In order to take your first steps into the third dimension, you'll need to understand VRML's structure and syntax. This chapter introduces you to the basic characteristics of the language, taking you through a description of the VRML file format; an explanation of nodes, including their properties and behaviors; and concludes with an overview of some of the important variable types and primitives built into VRML.

VRML's Basic Characteristics

VRML is primarily a way to group objects together. Derived from SGI's Open Inventor graphics library and file format, VRML's particular focus happens to be 3-D graphical objects. These objects could actually contain any type of data and as we will see, VRML's extensibility depends upon this.

Since the language deals with objects, it stands to reason that VRML is an object-oriented programming language. VRML's objects, called *nodes*, can contain virtually any type of information, and can have *children*. Nodes may also be reused through *instancing*. In order to provide a simple way for nodes to affect each other, VRML departs from the typical object-oriented language's tendency to make its individual components nonlinear, or randomly organized. A VRML source file, by contrast, resides in a *scene graph*, the hierarchical file that dictates the sequential order in which nodes must be parsed. This lets programmers control the order in which a scene is rendered and provides more precise controls over appearance and layout of scenes.

This said, a concise description of VRML might be formulated as follows: VRML is an object-oriented, 3-D graphics modeling language whose source scripts are interpreted linearly, from the beginning of the file to the end, in order to render a scene.

Object-Oriented Languages

Object-oriented programming languages, operating systems, and applications environments abound these days, but the status of "household word" has so far eluded the central concepts of object-oriented computing.

There are a host of features that may or may not be implemented in any given application of object-oriented thinking, but the basic concept remains consistent. In any object-oriented environment, the basic unit is a uniform, reusable container of information: an *object*.

In programming terms, this means that self-contained portions of code, previously referred to as procedures, subroutines, or functions, may now be referred to as objects. Objects can either be created from scratch or defined as *instances* of other objects. Instances are copies of objects that can be modified without changing the original and that *inherit* the attributes of the original. Inheritance is a powerful idea because it allows for the efficient reuse of code fragments.

Continued

Another object-oriented concept is that of *parent/child*. This refers to the relationship between an original object and a copy of that object, or to an object that contains other objects. VRML, for example, uses these terms in the latter fashion. In either case, the terms *parent* and *child* refer to an interaction between objects.

Control Structure Concepts—State and Separators

Linearity is crucial to the ability of one node to affect another's *state*. For example, a node that describes a light source will affect all nodes that follow it. This effect on a node's state can be limited through the use of the *separator*—one of VRML's two control structures. This performs a *push* and a *pop* on the current state, effectively separating the separator and all its contents from the rest of the scene graph.

Upon encountering a separator, the push saves the current state of the scene graph into memory. The object children of the separator are traversed, or interpreted, with nodes being drawn or changing the state of subsequent nodes. When the end of the separator is encountered, the pop causes the saved state to be restored for the continued traversal of the scene graph.

The other control structure is a *simple group*, which occurs whenever a node contains children nodes. It does not perform any operations on the current state, allowing it to traverse all the objects unaltered.

Once we have introduced some of VRML's defined nodes, you will see examples of both kinds of control structures.

Nodes

It stands to reason that if everything in a VRML scene graph is a node object, the design specification for a node must allow tremendous flexibility, and this is certainly the case. A node has a loose collection of characteristics that it must have and, in some cases, guidelines for the manner in which these characteristics can be expressed. These properties are as follows:

- The object type. Version 1.0 of the VRML specification defines 36 nodes, and the mechanisms by which other nodes may be defined in the future. Currently, nodes can be actual shapes or things that affect the way these shapes are drawn, such as a texture, a light source, an angle of rotation, or some kind of graphical transformation.

- The variables with parameters that describe size, color, rotation, or any other characteristic with a range of possible values. These variables are referred to in VRML as *fields*, and a node can have zero or more fields.

- The node's name. This is optional and a node will function without one. However, possessing a name adds tremendous power and flexibility to a node and to your scene as a whole. It makes a node reusable, for one thing, as well as providing a way to manipulate the object either within the VRML source or from the outside. If you do name a node, it need not be unique, but it must be the only name the node possesses.

- Some nodes may have children nodes, or other objects that are entirely contained within the parent node. This type of node is called a group node, and it will traverse its children linearly when the scene is being read and rendered. A group node can have zero or more children. As mentioned above, such a grouping does not perform a push and pop on the scene's state when it is traversed. It is primarily used to describe complex objects composed from many primitives.

The nodes defined by VRML V1.0 can be divided into three classes: *shape*, *property*, or *group*. Shape nodes are the only objects in VRML that actually cause an object to appear in the scene. Property nodes affect the way these shapes will be drawn in the scene, and include elements such as lighting and materials. Group nodes organize and associate nodes by containing them. A group node and all its children are treated as a single object. Some types of group nodes can also control whether a child node will be drawn.

Coordinate System

Using the typical mathematical representation of 3-D space, VRML expresses its world in terms of the x-, y-, and z-axes in a Cartesian projection. The positive z-axis projects into the viewing plane; the negative z-axis out, towards the viewer. The x-axis lies on the bottom of the viewing plane, and its positive axis projects to the right. The positive y-axis begins at the bottom of the viewing plane on the left-hand side and projects upwards. The origin (0, 0, 0) therefore lies at the bottom left-hand corner of the user's viewing plane.

The standard unit of measure for scale is the meter, with lengths and distances being expressed in this way. Angles are expressed in terms of radians, rather than the more familiar degree.

Radians Versus Degrees

We recognize that the sands of time tend to wear away the foundation of mathematical knowledge we acquired in college and high school, and so as a public service we now present a quick refresher course on geometry.

The angle around the circumference of a circle is familiar to us all as 360 degrees. In radians, this is expressed in terms of a measurement of the arc of a circle, defined by the angle of the radii that define the start and end of the arc. One radian equals an arc whose length matches the radius of a circle—there are exactly 2π radians in the circumference of a circle (the circumference of a circle is equal to 2π times the radius). Thus a radian equals approximately 57.295° (or $360/2\pi$). Using radians makes it easy to precisely describe arcs for angles of rotation and orientation, which is why they're used in VRML.

Syntax and File Structure

In the sections that follow, we'll examine the syntax and file structure for VRML.

The VRML File Format

Every file containing VRML source code must start with the line:

```
#VRML V1.0 ascii
```

This flags the browser about the contents and format of the file that follows.

Any line that begins with the pound sign (#) will be ignored by the browser and treated as a comment line. These comments may not be preserved by the server that delivers the document to the browser, which may also be configured to ignore comment lines during reading.

Whitespace in VRML code that is not required for parsing may likewise be removed from the file before it's transmitted over the network. Following the single identifying line, the file contains a single VRML node. This node may be a group node that contains an arbitrarily large number of children.

The file suffix for a VRML file is ".wrl", a contraction of "world" established as a naming convention in Version 1.0 of the VRML specification. At least two other sources advocate the use of the suffix ".vrml", a more meaningful and logical extension given that HTML files are almost universally saved with the suffix ".html".

It certainly would be trivial to configure an *HTTP* server to serve either as a VRML document, given the appropriate "mime.types" configurations. It would be preferable if the community could standardize around one naming convention, of course, but given the schism between 8×3 naming and the long names camp, this may or may not happen. The best of both worlds is to attempt to standardize on ".wrl" as laid out in the specification but to continue the use of ".vrml" where the author prefers it. This is analogous to the current situation with ".html" and ".htm".

Nodes, Again

Since we now know what a node is and what properties it possesses, let's look at the specific syntactical specifications for a node. A node is represented by a straightforward definition statement:

```
[DEF objectname] objecttype { [fields] [children]}
```

The only required portions of the definition are the type declaration and the curly braces. The name, fields, and children are optional. The keyword "DEF" must be prepended to the node if you are specifying a name.

The name of a node must not begin with a digit and must not contain control characters, spaces, single or double quotes, backslashes, curly braces, plus signs, or periods.

The syntax for the node's fields is the name of the field followed by the value. Fields are separated from each other and their values by whitespace. If a field may have multiple values, these values are enclosed in square brackets and separated by commas.

A simple example is the Cube node, which has three fields: *width*, *depth*, and *height*. This could be expressed as:

```
DEF MyCube Cube { width 3.3 depth 1.67 height 3.14 }
```

The order of the fields doesn't matter. If a field is omitted, a reasonable default value should be provided in the node that originally defined this object type, and this default will be used.

A node's children follow the same syntax as their parent. In fact, a node declared anywhere in the VRML document would follow this same simple syntax.

Variables, Properties, Groups, and Shapes

Field Types

A wide array of mathematical operations are required to render objects in three dimensions, and these operations require a large number of data types. VRML borrows the most critical of these data types, or *fields,* from Open Inventor's inventory of 42 different varieties.

The 16 field types defined in VRML V1.0 all fall into two general classes: single-value and multiple-value fields. Any single value may be a number (real or integer), Boolean, vector, or image. The naming convention for fields is to prefix all single value fields with the letters "SF" and all multiple value fields with "MF".

Valid Single-Value Field Types

SFBitMask This field has a bit flag that can be flipped through its various states through use of mnemonic names. The names are defined when the field is first created. An example would be a Cone node, which has an SFBitMask called "parts" that has bitmasks named "ALL", "SIDES", and "BOTTOM". The value can be set when the user creates a child Cone, and will determine how other nodes affect it.

SFBool A simple Boolean variable that may be written either numerically or as a string; i.e., "0" and "FALSE" are equivalent, as are "1" and "TRUE".

SFColor A simple, single-value method to express a color. The field contains a "triple"—three numbers in a single value. These three numbers range from 0.0 to 1.0, and represent red, green, and blue, respectively.

SFEnum A field that contains values for an enumerated type. These commonly define mnemonic labels for the values.

SFFloat A single-precision floating-point number written in scientific notation.

SFImage This is the field type used to store a bit-mapped image in VRML. The format for the field is to write three integers representing the width, height, and number of parts that the image possesses. This is followed by hexadecimal values in quantities equaling width multiplied by height and separated by whitespace.

The image is an uncompressed bitmap, with each component of the image (usually one pixel) being represented as intensities of color. A monochrome image would represent each pixel with a single byte where 0x00 is no intensity and 0xFF is the highest intensity ("0x" denotes hexadecimal representation).

Color pixels would have one byte each for red, green, and blue. A fourth byte may be added to represent transparency, with a value of 1.0 completely transparent and 0.0 completely opaque. The data must begin at the bottom left-hand corner and terminate at the top right-hand corner of the image.

Here's an example from the 1.0 specification:

```
2 4 3 0xFF0000 0xFF00 0 0 0 0 0xFFFFFF 0xFFFF00
```

This represents an image 2 pixels wide by 4 pixels high. The bottom-left pixel is red, the bottom-right pixel green, the two middle rows of pixels black, the top-left pixel is white, and the top-right pixel is yellow.

SFLong This is a field containing a single 32-bit integer. It may be written as decimal, hexadecimal (0x), or octal (beginning with 0).

SFMatrix This field type is used to represent a transformation matrix. It is written as 16 real numbers separated by whitespace and read as row-major order.

For example, a matrix expressing a translation of 7.3 units along the x-axis is written as:

```
1 0 0 0  0 1 0 0  0 0 1 0  7.3 0 0 1
```

SFRotation Used to represent an arbitrary rotation, this field type is represented by four floating-point values separated by whitespace. The first three values represent the axis of rotation, and the final value is the amount of right-handed rotation about that axis, in radians. For example, a 180 degree rotation about the x-axis is written as:

```
1 0 0  3.14159265
```

SFString A sequence of ASCII characters, also known as a string. If the string contains any whitespace, it must be prefaced and followed by double quotes. Any characters, including newlines, may appear in the string. A double quote may be included in the string by escaping it with a backslash, for example:

```
"Jonah \"Guts\" Bloomberg"
```

SFVec2f Contains a 2-D vector written as a pair of floating-point values. The values represent the direction and distance the vector travels from the current point.

SFVec3f Contains a 3-D vector represented as three floating-point values separated by whitespace. The extra value is needed to express the vector's direction in 3-D space.

Valid Multiple-Value Field Types

We have seen that perhaps the characterization "single value" is a misnomer, since many of the preceding value types were made up of an arbitrary number of individual parameters. What actually differentiates single-value from multiple-value field types in VRML is the latter's ability to describe or act upon more than one property or object. While *SFColor* can describe only a single color, its multiple value counterpart, *MFColor,* can define any number of color values. These values can then be referenced or bound to other objects by virtue of their position in the list of values.

The differences between single- and multiple-value field types can be likened to the difference between a single record and an array of records. A single record can contain any number of values and types of data, much like *SFImage* can contain information pertaining to the size and contents of an arbitrarily large bitmap. However, an array of records may contain any number of individual records that can be referred to by their index.

Later on we will examine when multiple-value fields are used and what impact they have on the description of a scene. That said, let's review the valid multiple-value field types.

MFColor   This field type contains any number of RGB colors. The colors are written as three floating-point numbers representing red, green, and blue, separated by whitespace. When there is more than one color value, the values are separated from each other by commas, and the entire field is enclosed in square brackets. For example, the field values:

```
[ 1 0 0, 0.0 1.0 0.0, 0 0 1 ]
```

represent red, green, and blue, respectively.

MFLong   Any number of long, or 32-bit, integers may be contained in a field of this type. The integers may be written in decimal, hexadecimal, or octal format. As with the *MFColor* type and all other multiple-value types, when there are two or more values present, commas are used to separate them and the entire field is surrounded by square brackets.

MFVec2f   This field type contains any number of 2-D vectors. The vectors are represented in the same way as their single-value counterparts, described previously.

MFVec3f   Three-dimensional vectors also have a multiple-value field type, with the now familiar syntax and the same rules of representation as the *SFVec3f* field type.

VRML Nodes, Part Three in 3-D

The field types we have just discussed form the foundation of VRML. Using them, virtually any type of 3-D object can be described. The actual rendering of a scene depends upon the definition and instancing of nodes and certain built-in assumptions and behaviors in VRML. These assumptions include concepts such as material or texture binding, bounding boxes, and viewing volumes.

The authors of the VRML specification included a number of the most useful nodes for the creation of a world. There are 36 of these objects, divided into four groups: geometries, properties, group nodes, and WWW nodes. We will explore some of these nodes, which will provide an opportunity to discuss the assumptions and behaviors that we've mentioned.

Simple Geometry Nodes

Also referred to as *shape nodes*, geometry nodes include AsciiText, Cone, Cube, Cylinder, IndexedFaceSet, IndexedLineSet, PointSet, and Sphere.

AsciiText The format of AsciiText is:

```
AsciiText {
    string          ""      # MFString - the actual text to be shown
    spacing         1       # SFFloat - multiplied against the height
                            # of the text to find the amount to
                            # advance the y-axis coordinate
                            # from one line to the next
    justification   LEFT    # SFEnum - LEFT, CENTER or RIGHT justified
    width           0       # MFFloat - any value other than zero will
                            # constrain the text to the width of the
                            # value. Zero indicates the
                            # text should be allowed to span its nat
                            # ural width.
}
```

In this definition, the default values for each field are noted to the right of the name of the field. In VRML, if an instance of a node does not specify values for all the fields in the node definition, it inherits the default values from that definition.

An instance of this type of node looks like:

```
DEF Title AsciiText { string    "Example of the \"AsciiText\" node"
        height    1
        justified CENTER
    }
```

Since we do not specify a value for "width", the definition's default value of zero is used instead.

The text in the node is affected by any transformations in the current state. Any nodes that precede nodes of this and most other types will affect the way this node is drawn. For AsciiText, the most important node that can affect its appearance is the FontStyle node, but any node that changes lighting or the current material can change the appearance of the AsciiText node.

If there is a texture currently defined, it will be applied to the text from the first line's point of origin to the right and upward along each character.

Cone The Cone node is defined as being, by default, centered at (0,0,0) and extends one unit of measure in all directions. That is, its height from base to apex is 2 units, and its radius is 1 unit. The apex of the cone is at (0,1,0) and its base is centered at (0,-1,0). It is defined as having two parts—its sides and its base or bottom.

The definition of parts becomes increasingly important as we begin to define primitive shapes that we want to bind materials or textures to. Defining the parts of a shape allow us greater control over which texture gets applied where, for example.

The various binding behaviors in VRML will be discussed later in this chapter. For now, assume the following: one or more available *materials* are applied to, or *bound to*, the shape being drawn according to the currently defined behavior. In general, they are applied either one per surface or one for the entire shape. The same applies to textures and *normals*. In the case of the cone, if the current binding behavior cycles through parts, it will bind to the sides first and the bottom second.

Normals: Imagine a Ray of Light

Normal is a term you will hear often in the 3-D graphics field. One of the most crucial aspects of high-quality computer graphics is getting the light right in the reflections and shading of the objects being rendered. A tremendous amount of work has been done on the algorithms and theoretical aspects of this problem. One of the common techniques used in calculating the effects of light sources on a scene are normals. These are vectors that run perpendicular to the surface of an object, and are used to estimate the light reflecting off the surface and back at the viewer.

The shape, like all others, is affected by the current cumulative transformative state and is drawn with the current texture and material.

If a texture is available, it will be applied to the cone in the following manner. The sides will be wrapped counterclockwise (when seen from above) beginning at the back of the cone, or the portion farthest from the origin of the z-axis. The bottom has a circle of the texture applied to it, with the top edge of the texture closest to the origin of the z-axis. The origin of the z-axis is the two-dimensional plane upon which the scene is being rendered, usually a computer monitor.

The Cone node is defined as:

```
Cone {
    parts          ALL        # SFBitMask - used to determine whether
                              # VRML should draw the SIDES, BOTTOM, or
                              # ALL the parts of the cone.
    bottomRadius   1          # SFFloat - adjusts the size of the base
```

```
height        2          # SFFloat - adjusts the distance from
                         # the base to the apex.

}
```

Cube This node can represent a six-sided object with the sides meeting at right angles. "Cube" is somewhat of a misnomer, since the dimensions of the sides need not be equal. The default location of the shape is to be centered at (0,0,0) and to measure 2 units in all directions, extending from +1 to -1 on each of the three axes. The shape is rendered according to the current transformative state using the current texture and material.

The order in which materials will be bound to the cube is front, back, left, right, top, and bottom. Textures are applied whole to each side of the cube. On the sides, the texture is applied right side up. On the top, the bottom edge of the texture is on the front edge of the cube face. On the bottom, the top edge of the texture is aligned on the front edge of the cube.

The Cube node is defined as:

```
Cube {
    width    2      # SFFloat
    height   2      # SFFloat
    depth    2      # SFFloat
    }
```

Cylinder This shape node is also centered around (0,0,0) and extends one unit in all directions. The cylindrical part runs vertically along the y-axis. The shape has three parts: the top, bottom, and sides. The shape is rendered according to the current transformative state using the current texture and material.

The order in which materials are bound to the shape's parts is: sides, top, then bottom. A texture is applied to the cylinder in much the same way as it was to the cone. Starting at the back of the cylinder, the texture is wrapped counterclockwise (when viewed from above) around the sides, terminating in a vertical seam at the back. On the caps at the top and bottom, circles are cut from the texture and these circles are applied. The bottom edge of the texture lies at the front edge of the cylinder at the top, and the top edge of the texture lies at the front edge at the bottom.

The Cylinder node is defined as:

```
Cylinder {
    parts    ALL    # SFBitMask - determines whether the browser
                    # should draw the SIDES, TOP, BOTTOM, or ALL the
                    # cylinder's parts
    radius  1       # SFFloat
    height  2       # SFFloat
    }
```

Sphere Spheres are represented by a node possessing only one field: the length of the radius. The default length is one unit, and the sphere is centered at the origin (0,0,0) unless otherwise positioned. The shape is rendered according to the current transformative state using the current texture and material.

Having no parts or sides, a sphere ignores the current binding behaviors for materials and textures. Instead it uses the first available material and applies it to itself using its own self-generated normals. If a texture is to be applied to the sphere, it will wrap the entire shape, starting from the back of the sphere and proceeding counterclockwise, in the same manner as the cylinder.

The Sphere node is defined as:

```
Sphere {
   radius  1       # SFFloat
     }
```

More Complex Shape Nodes

Now that we've gotten our feet wet with the shape primitives, we should have a fairly good idea of how field types are used in defining the parameters necessary to describe a shape mathematically. However, a 3-D scene that approaches photorealism is not going to be built of only cones, cubes, and spheres. The following polygonal shapes leap into a higher level of complexity. Polygonal modeling is the most efficient and popular method for drawing realistic, natural shapes. Everything from the human face to mountain ranges have been rendered using polygons, and they are a natural choice for VRML's graphical vocabulary.

IndexedFaceSet Implemented from Open Inventor, the IndexedFaceSet is the most commonly occurring geometry in Inventor-generated scenes. It represents a 3-D shape constructed from polygonal faces that in turn are defined by a series of *vertices*, or coordinate points. Taking the current location as its origin, the vertices are located one by one, the *coordIndex* field specifying the index of each coordinate, with an index of -1 signifying the end of a face.

The indices in *coordIndex* point to coordinate triples as defined by a preceding Coordinates3 node. The Coordinates3 node falls under the classification of property node, and acts like an array of points in three-dimensional space numbered zero through n, where n equals the number of points defined minus one.

As was the case with the less complex shape nodes, the vertices are rendered according to the current transformative state and use the current texture and material.

The default behavior for material binding on instances of IndexedFaceSet nodes is for one material to be bound on all *faces*. This can be overridden by the current state to change for each face according to the order specified by the node's *materialIndex* or *normalIndex*. If no such index is defined, the faces will just be cycled through in the order they are defined.

This type of error checking is common throughout VRML, whose architects attempted to take every possible measure to make sure a scene graph would be successfully traversed. Another example of this occurs with texture mapping on an instance of the IndexedFaceSet. Coordinates for binding textures to vertices can be explicitly defined using another node called TextureCoordinate2 and the indices in the *textureCoordIndex* field. However, if a texture is currently defined but no texture coordinates exist, a "best guess" is arrived at using the shape's bounding box and the texture is applied accordingly.

Bounding Boxes in 3-D Graphics

VRML calculates the bounding box of every defined shape node on-the-fly. It is calculated by taking the farthest point from the center of the object along each axis and using these points to create a cube. This cube completely envelops the object, and can be used for all kinds of calculations and transformations, including texture mapping and object culling, or deciding whether an object will be displayed given the volume of the current viewing area.

Similarly, normals may be specified for IndexedFaceSet objects or will be generated automatically. A final note on error correction vis-à-vis the IndexedFaceSet: if the indices contained in *coordIndex*, *materialIndex*, *normalIndex,* and *textureCoordIndex* are not valid in the context of the scene graph's current state, errors can occur.

The IndexedFaceSet node is defined as:

```
IndexedFaceSet {
    coordIndex           0  # MFLong - listing of indices that define
                            # the coordinates of the polygonal faces.
                            # An index of -1 indicates
                            # the end of one face and the beginning
                            # of another.
    materialIndex       -1  # MFLong - listing of indices that define
                            # the materials used on each polygon's
                            # vertices
    normalIndex         -1  # MFLong - defines the indices of the
                            # normals that will be applied to the
                            # shape
    textureCoordIndex   -1  # MFLong - indicates the coordinates each
                            # of the current textures will be bound
                            # to, also using an index
}
```

The preceding definition is undoubtedly too obtuse for all its parts to be clear. An example may help, and the following is a fragment of Gavin Bell's early draft of the VRML V1.0 specification, with our comments added for elucidation.

Sometimes, You Have to Start in the Middle

There will be some elements in the code fragment we have not visited yet, so please bear with us. VRML is a complex, highly interconnected language, and it is impossible to walk through it in a completely linear fashion.

In order to understand an object as complex as the IndexedFaceSet, we need to bring in other VRML nodes that act upon it and that it acts upon. If we wait until we introduce those other elements in detail to use them in examples, we will have left IndexedFaceSet unexplained for a very long time, and the initial window of understanding will have closed. We believe it is better to partially immerse you in actual working code, even with some elements that are foreign to you, than to march through the entire language in a dry, academic, linear fashion.

Here's the example:

```
Separator { # beginning of a separated object. Our state is now
clear
   Coordinate3 {
     point [ -1  1  1,  -1 -1  1,  1 -1  1,  1  1  1,
             -1  1 -1,  -1 -1 -1,  1 -1 -1,  1  1 -1 ]
   }
# we now have an indexed list of coordinates that define the eight
# points of a cube centered around (0,0,0) and extending 1 unit in
# all directions

Material { diffuseColor [ 1 0 0, 0 1 0, 0 0 1, 1 1 0 ] }
# the preceding defines indices 0, 1, 2, and 3 of our current
# colors. The materials are red, green, blue, and yellow,
# respectively (yellow being equal parts of red and green on the
# subtractive
# color wheel)

NormalBinding { value PER_FACE_INDEXED }
# this sets the binding behavior for normals

MaterialBinding { value PER_VERTEX_INDEXED }
# sets the binding behavior for the materials defined above

IndexedFaceSet {
# note we aren't naming any of these nodes, so the "DEF" keyword
# isn't required

   coordIndex [ 0, 1, 2, 3, -1, 3, 2, 6, 7, -1,
# front and back faces of a cube
        7, 6, 5, 4, -1, 4, 5, 1, 0, -1,  # back and left faces
        0, 3, 7, 4, -1, 1, 5, 6, 2, -1 ] # top and right faces
# note that these values are indices that refer to the coordinates
# in the "Coordinates3" node above, which defines points with
# indices numbered 0 through 7.

materialIndex [ 0, 0, 1, 1, -1,
# this index controls which of our colored materials defined above
# are bound to our nodes vertices. The materials are bound by index
```

```
# number to the vertices of the cube in the order they were defined
# in the coordIndex field
    2, 2, 3, 3, -1,
    0, 0, 1, 1, -1,
    2, 2, 3, 3, -1,
    0, 0, 0, 0, -1,
    2, 2, 2, 2, -1 ]
  }
# end of IndexedFaceSet


  }
# end separator
```

Property Nodes

Having confused you no end, we will now endeavor to pick up the pieces and explain some of the enigmas from the preceding example. This brings us directly to the second major category of VRML's built-in nodes, those that define properties.

Coordinate3 We'll begin with the first new node introduced in the example, Coordinate3 which defines a set of 3-D points by their coordinates. This set can be referenced by each coordinate's index by subsequent IndexedFaceSet, IndexedLineSet, or PointSet nodes. Defining this node does not draw anything during rendering; it merely replaces the current coordinates in the scene graph's state for following nodes to use.

The Coordinate3 node is defined as:

```
Coordinate3 {
        point  0 0 0  # MFVec3f
   }
```

Material The next type we encountered was the Material node. This node defines the surface material properties that will be accessible to all shape nodes that follow it. The individual materials can be accessed by their index numbers.

The concept of a material is defined as the way light reflects off the object's surface, and Material defines several parameters to allow the easy implementation of various "looks." These parameters are ambient, diffuse, specular, and emissive colors; a shininess parameter; and a transparency value.

Binding a material to a shape requires the use of a MaterialBinding node, whose setting may be interpreted differently by the various shape nodes, depending on their built-in behaviors.

The Material node is defined as:

```
Material {
            ambientColor    0.2 0.2 0.2      # MFColor
            diffuseColor    0.8 0.8 0.8      # MFColor
            specularColor   0 0 0            # MFColor
            emissiveColor   0 0 0            # MFColor
            shininess       0.2              # MFFloat
            transparency    0                # MFFloat
    }
```

MaterialBinding   In order to apply, or *bind*, materials defined in the node above to your shapes, you must use a MaterialBinding node. The values specified in this node will determine what behavior or behaviors materials follow when being bound to any subsequent shapes in your scene graph.

Binding behaviors can be identified as acting on parts of a shape, or faces, or vertices. Bindings for faces and vertices are relevant only to those shapes that have faces and vertices. Additionally, bindings may be specified by the index of the material for each face, part, or vertex, to allow greater control, but this will work only with shapes that allow indexing. An example of this would be the IndexedFaceSet node, since it has a field named *materialIndex.*

When the current materials list specifies multiple values for multiple fields, for example, three values for *diffuseColor,* two for *emissiveColor,* and one for *shininess,* the values will be cycled through as they are bound to a shape. The period of this cycle will be the number of values in the field that has the most values (in this case, *diffuseColor,* with three). All the materials will be cycled through and when a field runs out of values, it will wait for the end of the current cycle to its first value. Here's an example:

Cycle:	0	1	2	3
diffuseColor	0	1	2	0
emissiveColor	0	1	1	0
shininess	0	0	0	0

37

You can see that cycle 3 is identical to cycle 0. In the case where only one material is needed, the first values defined in each of the fields (index number 0) is considered the base material.

The different binding behaviors defined are:

DEFAULT: Use the object's default binding behavior.

OVERALL: The base material is bound to the entire object.

PER_PART: The materials are cycled through for each part of the shape. The "parts" are defined in the node's definition.

PER_PART_INDEXED: The materials are bound to each part by index, as specified in the shape node. That is, the shape node contains a field such as IndexedFaceSet's *materialIndex*, that specifies the indices of the materials to be bound to each part.

PER_FACE: A material is bound to each face of object, and cycling occurs in the way described earlier.

PER_FACE_INDEXED: Again, one material is bound to each face, this time as specified by the indices as listed in the shape node instance.

PER_VERTEX: Materials are bound to each vertex of the shape. As we said, this only applies to shapes that possess vertices.

PER_VERTEX_INDEXED: Same as above, except the materials are specified by index rather than cycled through automatically.

The MaterialBinding node is defined as:

```
MaterialBinding {
    value   DEFAULT        # SFEnum
  }
```

Normal Using this node allows you to define a set of 3-D surface normal vectors that will be used by any subsequent vertex-based shapes in the scene graph. Normals are used to control the amount and angle of reflectivity on a surface. The node does not draw anything in the scene; it merely influences the overall look of its objects. If normals are not specified, they will be generated automatically by those shapes that require them, i.e., IndexedFaceSet, IndexedLineSet, and PointSet. The Normal node is defined as:

```
Normal {
     vector  0 0 1 # MFVec3f
   }
```

NormalBinding Like MaterialBinding, this node specifies the behavior of the current normals when they are bound to shapes that follow in the scene graph. Also like MaterialBinding, different shape nodes will treat these behaviors differently, depending on, among other factors, the ordering of their parts.

When you specify a display behavior that requires normals, be sure to supply the required number of vectors to elicit that behavior, or rendering errors will occur. Like MaterialBinding, the behaviors that deal with faces and vertices are only relevant to those shapes that have faces and vertices. Indexed bindings are only usable with shapes that allow for the use of indices.

The following defined binding behaviors are from the 1.0 specification:

DEFAULT: Use default binding.

OVERALL: Whole object has same normal.

PER_PART: One normal for each part of object.

PER_PART_INDEXED: One normal for each part, indexed.

PER_FACE: One normal for each face of object.

PER_FACE_INDEXED: One normal for each face, indexed.

PER_VERTEX: One normal for each vertex of object.

PER_VERTEX_INDEXED: One normal for each vertex, indexed.
The NormalBinding node is defined as:

```
NormalBinding {
    value   DEFAULT        # SFEnum
    }
```

Separator Finally, let's explore VRML's group nodes. We saw the Separator node at work in our example of the IndexedFaceSet, and we discussed it in our coverage of control structures, but its characteristics are worth reiterating.

The importance of the Separator node in VRML scenes cannot be overstated, since it is effectively the only control structure that allows for the isolation of pieces of code from other pieces. When encountered, the Separator node causes the current traversal state to be pushed (saved in memory) before its children are read and rendered. Effectively, this gives the Separator's children a clean slate from which to work. When the end of the Separator is reached, the scene graph's state is popped (retrieved from memory) and the previous state replaces any property changes that the Separator's children may have introduced.

Additionally, Separator nodes have a feature called *render culling.* This is a powerful tool that allows the children of the node to be skipped over during traversal, based on a calculation of the Separator's bounding box compared to the current view volume. The Separator has a setting to disallow or force render culling, and the actual behavior is controlled by the VRML viewer/renderer.

The Separator *node* is defined as:

```
Separator {
            renderCulling          AUTO
# SFEnum - AUTO allows the viewer to decide whether to cull or not.
# The other values defined are ON or OFF, which force the viewer to
# either cull or not.
    }
```

Group The simplest of group nodes, this represents the base class for the rest of the group nodes. Group contains an ordered list of child nodes. This list is traversed linearly, cannot perform render culling, and does not perform a push and pop on the traversal state. It can be viewed as a logical association of nodes that are related in some way.

The Group node is defined as:

```
Group {
   }
```

Switch A powerful control structure when manipulating VRML scenes with scripts or programs, this group node can be instructed to traverse one, none, or all of its children. If controlled by a variable condition from some external source (e.g., a Perl script or other CGI-type tool), it can be used to widely vary the contents of the scene or their properties.

The field named *whichChild* specifies the index of the child node that will be traversed. The children are numbered sequentially, starting with zero. A value of -1 is the default, and signifies that none of the children should be traversed. A value of -3 will cause all of the group's children to be traversed, and the Switch will behave exactly as a Group node.

The Switch node is defined as:

```
Switch {
    whichChild   -1        # SFLong
   }
```

Summary

Starting with the basic concepts of the language—the linear traversal of a sequence of nodes that contain information on shapes or properties—we then moved on to the building blocks of the language. The field types were listed and explained, and then we began our exploration of VRML's built-in nodes. In describing various node types, we touched on some of VRML's intermediate concepts such as binding behavior, normals, vertices, polygons, and traversal state. We hope that we have imparted not only an understanding of the language's underpinnings, but also inspired some ideas about how to use VRML in the real world.

From looking at the source code, you can easily see that VRML is not meant to be constructed by hand, line by line. We anticipate that 99% of such code will be generated by development tools (world builders, if you will) and then tweaked by hand. This tweaking, to be done properly, requires a full understanding of the workings of all parts of VRML. Only when armed with the knowledge of concepts such as node naming, switch groups, render culling, and the like will you be able to manipulate scenes on-the-fly to add some of the interactivity that VRML currently lacks.

In the next chapter, we'll continue our trek through the 1.0 specification, moving through some more advanced nodes and concepts, and finally cleaning up the miscellaneous pieces that we've skipped along the way. As you see the rest of the components, keep in mind the possibilities VRML has for development, extensibility, and programmability.

CHAPTER 3

Advanced VRML
The Saga Continues

*V*RML is a complex language and what we've covered so far has really only scratched the surface. To complete what we started in the last chapter, we'll begin by cleaning up some miscellaneous shape and property nodes.

From there, we'll dive into textures and some other advanced property nodes. Next, we'll introduce VRML's various light and camera nodes, the methods by which your scenes will be revealed to their viewers. Finally, we'll close with some features of VRML that were born out of the particular needs of serving scenes from decentralized computers over a variable bandwidth network.

Final Shapes

In order to complete what we began in Chapter 2 with our introduction to shape nodes, we need to look at the final two shapes defined in the VRML 1.0 specification.

IndexedLineSet Like IndexedFaceSet, the IndexedLineSet node represents a way of describing a shape with an arbitrary number of polygons. Unlike the IndexedFaceSet, these polygons do not have solid faces; instead they are a collection of simple lines. The polygons are constructed from vertices located at the current set of 3-D coordinates.

43

The *coordIndex* field defines the order of coordinates used by their indices, with an index of -1 indicating the end of the current polygon.

A quick example is appropriate, since the concept of indexed values of various types is so central to VRML. The following VRML fragment will demonstrate the use of indexed coordinates:

```
Coordinates3 {0 0 0, 0 1 0, 1 1 0, 1 0 0,
              0 0 -1, 0 1 -1, 1 1 -1, 1 0 -1}
# eight points that will be used to describe a cube, now stored
# in the indices 0 through 7


IndexedLineSet {
    coordIndex [ 0, 1, 2, 3, -1, # front of shape, i.e., the square
                                  # whose bottom left-hand corner is
                                  # at 0,0,0 and whose top
                                  # right-hand corner is at 1,1,0
                 0, 1, 5, 4, -1, # left side of shape
                 4, 5, 6, 7, -1, # back of shape
                 3, 2, 6, 7, -1, # right side of shape
                 0, 4, 7, 3, -1 ]# bottom of shape
```

The current transformative state of the scene graph will be applied to the node when it is parsed and rendered. The defined behaviors for material and normal binding are:

- PER_PART binds a material or normal to each segment of the line.
- PER_FACE binds materials or normals to each polyline, or all the lines that make up one polygonal shape.
- PER_VERTEX binds materials or normals to each vertex.
- The DEFAULT behavior is OVERALL for materials and PER_VERTEX_INDEXED for normals.

Two issues to note: if insufficient normals are supplied for the number of vertices, the object will be drawn unlit. Secondly, the normal and material bindings listed above are the same for the _INDEXED counterparts to the values listed above. In other worlds, PER_FACE_INDEXED would act the same as PER_FACE, except the values to be bound would be supplied by the *materialIndex* or *normalIndex* indices.

Finally, textures may be applied to the lines in the same way they are to IndexedFaceSet.

The IndexedLineSet node is defined as:

```
IndexedLineSet {
          coordIndex          0 # MFLong
          materialIndex       -1 # MFLong
          normalIndex         - 1 # MFLong
          textureCoordIndex   -1 # MFLong
     }
```

PointSet Using this node, you can represent a series of points located at a subset of the currently defined coordinates. This subset is defined by the index of the starting coordinate and the number of points in the set. Given this information, VRML defines the first point at the coordinates of the starting index and then creates a point at each coordinate in sequence until the total number of points are created.

The current transformative state affects this node's properties as it does almost all shape nodes. A single material is, by default, bound to the entire set. If the _MaterialBinding_ is set to PER_PART, PER_FACE, or PER_VERTEX, one material is bound to each point successively.

Normal binding is handled by default the PER_VERTEX way, with one normal bound to each point's vertex.

The PointSet node is defined as:

```
PointSet {
          startIndex  0 # SFLong - specifies the coordinate to
                        # start with. If PER_VERTEX bindings are in
                        # effect, it also specifies the
                        # normal and material to start with.


          numPoints   -1 # SFLong - number of points in the
                         # set. The value of -1 indicates that all
                         # remaining currently
                         # defined coordinates should be used.
     }
```

Property Nodes

With the shapes finally out of the way, we're free to turn to the nodes that affect the way shapes are drawn. The property nodes we introduced in Chapter One defined materials, normals, and coordinates, and dictated the way these properties would be implemented in the scene graph.

Miscellany

In the following pages, we'll visit nodes that define text formats, object placement and orientation, textures, lights, and cameras. To begin with, we'll cover a handful of property nodes that don't group easily into any specific category.

FontStyle The format and style of all AsciiText nodes can be influenced through the use of the FontStyle node. Like HTML, VRML does not define specific typefaces, merely the styles. It is left to the browser program to translate "SERIF," for example, into Times Roman or Bookman. The size is measured in scene object units, usually meters, and is used to calculate the text's height and the line spacing. (A point is a typographical measure more commonly used to measure text height and line spacing; it equals approximately 1/72 of an inch; in metric terms, therefore, a point equals 0.3525mm or 0.0003525m.)

The allowable values for the FontStyle fields are:

- *family*
  - — SERIF: serif typeface (i.e., Times Roman)
  - — SANS: sans serif typeface (i.e., Helvetica)
  - — TYPEWRITER: fixed-pitch typeface (i.e., Courier)
- *style*
  - — NONE: no modifications to family
  - — BOLD: make serif, sans serif, or typewriter bold
  - — ITALIC: make serif, sans serif, or typewriter italic or slanted

The default file format is:

```
FontStyle {
    size      10      # SFFloat
    family    SERIF   # SFEnum
    style     NONE    # SFBitMask
}
```

Info The Info node exists as a way to embed text strings into the fabric of a scene graph. The text does not appear anywhere in the scene, but it is available if a browser is looking for it. This may be formalized in the future to serve some type of document, copyright, or creator information. The Info node is defined as:

```
Info {
     string   "<Undefined info>"      # SFString
}
```

Transformations

Our next batch of nodes affect the visual orientation or presentation of the shapes that follow them. Each property node that performs some kind of transformation is cumulative; that is, its effect is added to the effect of all preceding property nodes to create the tranformative state. This is an efficient way to break transformations down into steps where certain shapes are drawn or other actions performed.

Rotation If every shape node in a given scene sat exactly square on all three axes, VRML would not provide much of an illusion of realism. Tilting and skewing provide us with many of the cues we use to interpolate relative position and probable direction of movement—the Rotation node can be used to enliven an otherwise bland scene.

Rotation specifies the axis and amount of rotation (in radians). Each occurrence of Rotation in a scene graph is accumulated in the transformative state and therefore affects each eligible shape node that follows it.

The Rotation node is defined as:

```
Rotation {
     rotation  0  0  1  0    # SFRotation
}
```

Scale The use of this node allows for precise control of the scale of subsequent shapes along all three axes. The 3-D scale is expressed as a vector, with a floating-point integer for each axis, so that a non-uniform scale can be applied, if desired. Each value of the scaling vector is multiplied to the aspects of the shape to be scaled that fall upon the like axis. For example, a value of (2 2 2) would result in a 200% increase in the object's scale applied uniformly to all three axes, whereas a value of (2 1 1) would only increase the x-values for the object and leave the y- and z-axes unaltered.

The Scale node is defined as:

```
Scale {
        scaleFactor   1 1 1      # SFVec3f
}
```

Translation The term *translation* is used in 3-D graphics to describe a transformation on an object that occurs parallel to the coordinate axes; that is, that contains no rotation or scaling. In other words, it is a linear "move" transformation, with the 3-D vector describing the distance the object moves along each of the axes.

The Translation node is defined as:

```
Translation {
        translation  0 0 0      # SFVec3f
}
```

Transform With all the simple transforms we have discussed thus far, each node has been defined as performing a single action. What if we want to apply a number of different types of transforms at one time? We can either use instances of the individual nodes, or we can group all our transforms in a single node, named appropriately, Transform.

This node may contain one or more of the following: Translation, Scale, and Rotation. In addition, Transform adds a *center* field that changes the origin point in the current transformative state, and breaks Scale out into two separate fields, *scaleFactor* for amount of scale and *scaleOrientation* for orientation of scale. This modification allows more control than the regular Scale node.

The Transform node is defined as:

```
Transform {
        translation        0 0 0          # SFVec3f
        rotation           0 0 1 0        # SFRotation
        scaleFactor        1 1 1          # SFVec3f
        scaleOrientation   0 0 1 0        # SFRotation
        center             0 0 0          # SFVec3f
}
```

To further illustrate the use of the Transform node, the following example was furnished in the 1.0 specification.

This Transform node definition:

```
Transform {
    translation T1
    rotation R1
    scaleFactor S
    scaleOrientation R2
    center T2
}
```

is equivalent to the sequence:

```
Translation { translation T1 }
Translation { translation T2 }
Rotation { rotation R1 }
Rotation { rotation R2 }
Scale { scaleFactor S }
Rotation { rotation -R2 }
Translation { translation -T2 }
```

TransformSeparator With all this emphasis on the importance of transformations, it stands to reason that there would be a group node designed for them. Like the Separator node, the TransformSeparator saves the scene graph's state before traversing its children. However, this save, or *push* operation only affects the current transformation; the rest of the state is unaffected. In this way, an element such as a camera or light source can be positioned without its transformation affecting the rest of the scene, even though the object will persist throughout the remainder of the scene.

The TransformSeparator node is defined as:

```
TransformSeparator {
}
```

MatrixTransform Finally, the MatrixTransform node performs a classical geometric 3-D transformation using a four-by-four matrix. What this means is, given the following matrix:

```
1 0 0 0
0 1 0 0
0 0 1 0
0 0 0 1
```

the inner nine numbers, starting in the upper-left hand corner, are a rotation matrix, defining how far an object rotates around an axis:

```
1 0 0
0 1 0
0 0 1
```

The outer seven numbers are a translation matrix, describing how far an object moves along an axis:

```
       0
       0
       0
0 0 0 1
```

This can be summarized as:

```
[matrix of original object position] * [matrix of change in object
position] = [matrix of new object position]
```

The MatrixTransform node is defined as:

```
MatrixTransform {
     matrix  1 0 0 0        # SFMatrix
             0 1 0 0
             0 0 1 0
             0 0 0 1
}
```

Crunchy, Squishy, Sticky, or Slimy?

The next class of property nodes are those that define textures to be wrapped onto the surfaces of shape nodes. Without textures, VRML objects would be nothing more than a collection of flat, colored faces and lines with nice shading. Textures traditionally are relied upon in 3-D rendering to "fake" real objects and materials by shortcutting to the kind of complexity a real surface has. This is achieved by taking a two-dimensional image, either photographic or painted, and applying it to the drawn surface. In this way the texture appears to take on the shape of the object, and vice versa.

Texture2 The raw material for a texture map is specified in the Texture2 node. Any subsequent shape node that requires a texture will use the image and parameters specified here. An image is supplied by Texture2 either by pointing to a local file, supplying a URL to a Web-accessible file, or by embedding it directly in the node. If an empty string is specified as a filename, texturing will be turned off.

When speaking of textures, two special axes are defined for the directions in which the texture is applied to an object. These axes are named S and T. S is the horizontally oriented axis, and T is vertically oriented, but this definition is subject to variation since they do not necessarily have to fall on any of the Cartesian axes. The Texture2 node allows for control over the wrapping behavior of the texture as it is applied to each of the S and T axes.

The defined wrapping behaviors are:

- REPEAT: when the texture is applied to its full dimension, it will start over from its origin.

- CLAMP: this prevents wrapping beyond the size of the texture image.

The Texture2 node is defined as:

```
Texture2 {
        filename      ""          # SFString
        image         0 0 0       # SFImage
        wrapS         REPEAT      # SFEnum
        wrapT         REPEAT      # SFEnum
}
```

Texture2Transform In order to specify the way in which textures will be applied to surfaces, the Texture2Transform node contains fields that dictate _translation, rotation, scaleFactor,_ and _center._ Cumulatively, these fields define a 2-D transformation that is applied to the texture as it appears on all subsequent surfaces.

The Texture2Transform node is defined as:

```
Texture2Transform {
        translation   0 0         # SFVec2f
        rotation      0           # SFFloat
        scaleFactor   1 1         # SFVec2f
        center        0 0         # SFVec2f
}
```

TextureCoordinate2 In order to use textures with indexed shape nodes such as PointSet, IndexedLineSet, or IndexedFaceSet, a map must be created that matches a specific point in the texture to the appropriate indexed set. This mapping is performed using TextureCoordinate2 objects.

The coordinate pair consists of two numbers that range between 0 and 1 across the texture, with 0 being the origin of the axis and 1 being the furthest point the texture reaches on that axis. The S coordinate is listed first, with the T coordinate following.

The TextureCoordinate2 node is defined as:

```
TextureCoordinate2 {
     point  0 0     # MFVec2f
}
```

ShapeHints While not directly related to textures, ShapeHints do affect the appearance of the surfaces upon which textures are applied. ShapeHints can define IndexedFaceSets as containing ordered vertices, solid, or convex faces.

The addition of ShapeHints to a scene graph has the added benefit of allowing certain rendering optimizations that can lessen the overall render time. For example, the VRML viewer may implement various culls based on the visibility of back faces or alter the basic lighting characteristics for the same reasons. A specific example from the 1.0 specification is as follows:

> *...if an object is solid and has ordered vertices, an implementation may turn on backface culling and turn off two-sided lighting. If the object is not solid but has ordered vertices, it may turn off backface culling and turn on two-sided lighting.*

There are many other variations that could be implemented, depending on the scene's elements, the speed of the rendering machine's CPU, and the amount of network bandwidth available.

ShapeHints can also affect the way in which normals are generated for faces. If normals are not supplied in a given IndexedFaceSet, for instance, VRML mandates that normals will be generated for it to calculate the reflections of light off the object. ShapeHints contains a field named *creaseAngle* that helps generate normals by determining which edges should be beveled or smoothed, and which should be faceted, or sharply defined. This determination is made by comparing the value of *creaseAngle* to the actual angle between two adjacent polygons. If the angle between the two polygonal faces is less than the value of *creaseAngle,* the transition between the two will be smoothly shaded. The default value for *creaseAngle* is 0.5 radians, or about 30 degrees.

Finally, ShapeHints can specify an order to the faces of an object, overriding the default order as defined in the node itself. The options for this ordering are as follows:

- UNKNOWN_ORDERING: Ordering of vertices is unaltered from the default as defined in the node itself.
- CLOCKWISE: Face vertices are ordered clockwise starting from the furthest vertex from the origin.
- COUNTERCLOCKWISE: Face vertices are ordered counterclockwise, also starting with the furthest vertex from the origin.

The two remaining fields, *shapeType* and *faceType*, may be defined as UNKNOWN_SHAPE_TYPE, or they may take the values of SOLID and CONVEX, respectively.

The ShapeHints node is defined as:

```
ShapeHints {
    vertexOrdering  UNKNOWN_CRDERING      # SFEnum
    shapeType       UNKNOWN_SHAPE_TYPE    # SFEnum
    faceType        CONVEX                # SFEnum
    creaseAngle     0.5                   # SFFloat
}
```

Lights, Camera...

All the elements of VRML discussed thus far can be combined in a nearly infinite number of ways, to create a similarly large number of rooms, landscapes, objects, and general scenes. However, none of this will do anyone any good without some way to see it and, even more importantly, to vary the user's view of the scene. This is where camera and light nodes come in. VRML defines two camera and three light nodes, called OrthographicCamera, PerspectiveCamera, DirectionalLight, SpotLight, and PointLight. Each wields its own unique influence over the way a scene appears.

Bounding Boxes and Viewing Volume

From the previous chapter, we know that *bounding boxes* are defined as the smallest box shape that can contain an entire object. *Viewing volume* can be thought of as the largest bounding box that will fit into the current conditions, such as the viewer's position and distance from the scene graph, the type of camera, the size of viewing window, etc. Whether or not an object can be displayed in the view largely depends on a comparison of the current viewing volume and the object's bounding box.

Work with me, baby

In this part of our VRML discussion we'll introduce the notion of a defined point of view, known appropriately in graphics-speak as a *camera* or *camera-eye*.

OrthographicCamera An *orthographic* or *parallel projection* is one that translates a 3-D scene or object onto a 2-D plane without any perspective division (in other words, the size of objects is preserved).

A scene graph viewed through an OrthographicCamera node presents such a projection. The viewing volume of the camera is defined as a rectangular box, and objects do not diminish in size as they recede into the distance.

In VRML, if there is no camera defined in a scene, the default position for a node of this type is (0, 0, 1) (i.e., one meter from the 2-D projection surface), looking along the negative z-axis. OrthographicCamera has fields that can be used to adjust this initial position and orientation, as well as the height of the viewing volume.

Additionally, transformation nodes affect the camera nodes, so a translation, scale, or rotation effect could be placed just before the definition of the camera to further affect its initial properties.

By placing a camera in a scene, the architect of the scene takes ownership of the viewer's first look at the scene. That is, the defaults are overridden and a customized look is presented. From this starting point, the viewer software will typically allow the user to modify the camera and navigate around the scene.

The OrthographicCamera node is defined as:

```
OrthographicCamera {
        position        0 0 1           # SFVec3f
        orientation     0 0 1  0        # SFRotation
        focalDistance   5               # SFFloat
        height          2               # SFFloat
}
```

PerspectiveCamera A perspective projection differs from an orthographic projection—when the 3-D scene is translated onto the 2-D plane, perspective division does take place. In other words, objects do diminish as they travel farther from the camera. The PerspectiveCamera node describes such a view, and by virtue of this characteristic, has a viewing volume shaped like a truncated right pyramid.

The default location for the camera is the same as for OrthographicCamera, (0, 0, 1), looking along the negative z-axis. The field named *heightAngle* can be used to alter the total vertical angle of the viewing volume (and consequently the total viewing volume).

The camera's other defaults and characteristics match those of OrthographicCamera.

The PerspectiveCamera node is defined as:

```
PerspectiveCamera {
        position        0 0 1           # SFVec3f
        orientation     0 0 1  0        # SFRotation
        focalDistance   5               # SFFloat
        heightAngle     0.785398        # SFFloat
}
```

Painting on your cornea

In VRML, cameras serve as proxies for our eyes, but neither cameras nor eyes function very well in a pitch-black void. And so we come to the other half of the yin-yang of seeing—light.

PointLight The simplest of the light sources, PointLight defines an omnidirectional light emanating from a fixed 3-D location. Being omnidirectional, PointLight illuminates equally in all directions. Various fields define the location, color, and intensity of the light source.

Light nodes are affected by the scene graph's current transformative state, and may affect shapes whose instances follow it. A light source imbedded in a Separator node does not affect the appearance of any shapes that are defined outside that Separator.

The PointLight node is defined as:

```
PointLight {
        on          TRUE        # SFBool - a value of FALSE would
                                # "turn off" the light
        intensity   1           # SFFloat - 0 represents no
                                # intensity, 1 represents full
                                # intensity
        color       1 1 1       # SFColor
        location    0 0 1       # SFVec3f
}
```

DirectionalLight The DirectionalLight node offers the user a more precise control over the objects it affects. Instead of shedding light equally in all directions, DirectionalLight illuminates a path that is parallel to the 3-D vector defined in the node instance's *direction* field.

These rays run parallel and do not disperse as true light would. The illumination it provides is exactly as it is initially defined all the way to infinity. Also, because it exists as a vector and does not vary over its length, the source cannot be said to have any point of origin.

DirectionalLight's behavior inside a Separator, and its relationship with the current transformative state, are the same as for PointLight.

The DirectionalLight node is defined as:

```
DirectionalLight {
        on          TRUE        # SFBool
        intensity   1           # SFFloat
        color       1 1 1       # SFColor
        direction   0 0 -1      # SFVec3f
}
```

SpotLight For more control and realism, SpotLight is the way to go. A spotlight is a source located at a fixed three-dimensional coordinate whose illuminating rays are cast in a cone that runs along a 3-D vector.

Additionally, the intensity of the illumination diminishes exponentially as each ray moves farther from the center of the cone. There are fields to specify the drop-off rate and the angle of the cone.

The other default values and behaviors of SpotLight are the same as the behaviors common to PointLight and DirectionalLight.

The SpotLight node is defined as:

```
SpotLight {
        on            TRUE       # SFBool
        intensity     1          # SFFloat
        color         1 1 1      # SFVec3f
        location      0 0 1      # SFVec3f
        direction     0 0 -1     # SFVec3f
        dropOffRate   0          # SFFloat
        cutOffAngle   0.785398   # SFFloat - dictates the angle
                                 # between the 'direction' vector
                                 # and the edge of the cone in
                                 # radians
}
```

Internet-Specific Aspects of VRML

VRML is, simply, a file format designed for delivery and use of three-dimensional scenes and objects over the Internet. Obviously, the demands of this medium are going to shape the modeling language. In the 1.0 specification, there are some initial hints of this evolutionary adaptation, in the form of two features designed for interoperability with the World Wide Web, and one common 3-D rendering feature that is elevated to new importance.

WWWAnchor This is a group node that serves a function similar to an HTML link. When one of the WWWAnchor group's children is chosen, this node will cause a new VRML scene to be loaded. The implementation of this "choosing" action is dependent on the browser/viewer being used. As with HTML, the node suggests only what type of action should be taken, not how that action should take place or even how it should be triggered.

The new scene to be loaded is specified by the *name* field, which can contain a local file or a URL that points to an HTTP-accessible file on an arbitrary system. If the name field contains an empty string, choosing one of its children does nothing.

WWWAnchor is a group node in the same sense as the Separator node, in that it performs a push and a pop on the scene's current state to preserve it while its children are being traversed.

When the anchored file is opened via a URL, the coordinates of the point on the object can be passed along with the URL. This is achieved by setting the *map* field to POINT instead of its default value, NONE. The coordinates are sent by appending "?x,y,z" to the end of the URL. For example, if the *name* field has the value:

```
http://www.outer.net/vrml/sample.wrl
```

and the user chooses a child of the WWWAnchor group at the coordinate (4, 2.5, -4), then the URL will be requested from the HTTP server at *outer.net* as:

```
http://www.outer.net/vrml/sample.wrl?4,2.5,-4
```

You could use this capability to filter the resulting VRML through a script that can change the contents of the file according to the coordinate value.

Finally, there is a mechanism built into WWWanchor that allows for a meaningful name to be attached to the entire group. This is an improvement over the URL, which would otherwise be the only information available to display when the user asks where the group's children will lead to.

The WWWAnchornode is defined as:

```
WWWAnchor {
        name ""         # SFString
        description ""  # SFString - the alternate text to explain
                        # the group's destination.
        map NONE        # SFEnum - to pass the chosen coordinates,
                        # set this field to POINT; the group's #
                        # children would come here.
}
```

WWWInline This node may be the biggest factor that decides the success or failure of VRML in the mass market. The vast majority of its intended audience are operating on a personal computer over analog modem connections, and VRML's ability to scale up or down based on the available bandwidth and CPU resource is crucial. The WWWInline node allows a VRML scene graph's individual nodes to be stored as a series of separate files in one or more locations.

The children of the WWWInline node are retrieved from the specified URL when the viewer decides it needs them. This means that the software can make intelligent decisions that weigh all the various factors before deciding whether or not to transfer potentially vast quantities of data.

Additionally, if the inlined object is a shape node, its bounding box can be specified using the *bboxSize* and *bboxCenter* fields. This will allow further control to be wielded by the viewer, such as view-volume culling, before making the decision to retrieve the file.

Most interesting, perhaps, is the possibility that VRML's inlining capabilities may lead to a WWW-retrievable library of nodes, so that scenes can be created and rendered using "off-the-shelf" nodes that are near or even local to the viewing system.

The syntax for this node is:

```
WWWInline {
    name ""                 # SFString - an empty name causes no
                            # action whatsoever
    bboxSize 0 0 0          # SFVec3f
    bboxCenter 0 0 0        # SFVec3f
}
```

LOD LOD (Level-of-Detail) refers to a set of criteria used for a sophisticated form of culling. Essentially, it allows a viewing program to choose among a set of views of a single object based on the user's distance from the object.

If we were viewing a room with a painting on the wall, it may appear as a simple, solid-colored square as we are standing at the opposite wall. Move closer, and the square turns into three squares inside each other, to give the appearance of a frame and a crude circular shape inside the innermost square. Closer still, and it becomes a frame with a wood texture and a low-resolution bitmapped image. Right up in front

of the painting, we find ourselves looking at a 24-bit image of
Primavera in a mahogany and gold leaf frame.

The mechanism for performing this kind of magic is as follows: The
center of the LOD group is used to calculate the distance from the
viewing "eye" to the group of objects. The result is compared against an
array of distances. If it is smaller than the first value in this array, then
the first child of the LOD group is selected and rendered. If the value is
more than the first but less than the second value, the second child
node is selected, and so on.

From this we see that the children should begin with the most to the
least detailed version. Also, if there are n values in the array, we should
supply n+1 children in the group. If there is a shortage of children, the
last one will be used repeatedly until the range array is exhausted.

The LOD concept is especially powerful when combined with the
WWWInlining node. This is why we lumped LOD into the Internet-
specific elements of VRML. By itself, it provides a way to speed rendering times by jettisoning unnecessary detail. Combined with
WWWInlining, the children of the LOD group can exist on a remote
server until the viewer gets close enough to warrant retrieval and display. Furthermore, the decision to switch to the next level of detail
could be made, not solely on the basis of distance, but according to
factors such as Internet connection speed and computational power.

The LOD node is defined as:

```
LOD {
      range [ ]      # MFFloat
      center 0 0 0 # SFVec3f
}
```

Instancing A node may be the child of more than one group. This
is called *instancing* (using the same instance of a node multiple times,
called "aliasing" or "multiple references" in other systems), and is accomplished with the USE keyword.

The DEF keyword both defines a named node and creates a single
instance of it. The USE keyword indicates that the most recently
defined instance should be used again. If several nodes were given the
same name, then the last DEF encountered during parsing "wins."
DEF/USE is limited to a single file; there is no mechanism for USEing
nodes that are DEFed in other files.

A name goes into scope as soon as the DEF is encountered, and does not go out of scope until another DEF with the same name or the end-of-file are encountered. Nodes cannot be shared between files (you cannot USE a node that was DEFed inside the file to which a WWWInline refers).

For example, rendering this scene will result in three spheres being drawn; both named "Joe" and the second (smaller) sphere drawn twice:

```
Separator {

        DEF Joe Sphere { }
        Translation { translation 2 0 0 }
        Separator {

                DEF Joe Sphere { radius .2 }
                Translation { translation 2 0 0 }

        }
        USE Joe     # radius .2 sphere will be used here
```

Extensibility Extensions to VRML are supported via self-describing nodes. Nodes that are not part of standard VRML must first write out a description of their fields, so that all VRML implementations are able to parse and ignore their extensions.

This description is written just after the opening curly brace for the node, and consists of the keyword "fields" followed by a list of the types and names of fields used by that node, all enclosed in square brackets and separated by commas. For example, if Cube was not a standard VRML node, it would be written like this:

```
Cube {
   fields [ SFFloat width, SFFloat height, SFFloat depth ]
   width 10 height 4 depth 3
```

Specifying the fields for nodes that *are* part of standard VRML is not an error; VRML parsers must silently ignore these field specifications.

isA relationships A new node type may also be a superset of an existing node that is part of the standard. In this case, if an implementation for the new node type cannot be found, the new node type can be safely treated as the existing node it is based on (with some loss of functionality, of course). To support this, new node types can define an MFString field called *isA* containing the names of the types of which it is a superset. For example, a new type of Material called

ExtendedMaterial that adds an index of refraction as a material property would be written as:

```
ExtendedMaterial {
   fields [ MFString isA, MFFloat indexOfRefraction,
            MFColor ambientColor, MFColor diffuseColor,
            MFColor specularColor, MFColor emissiveColor,
            MFFloat shininess, MFFloat transparency ]
   isA [ "Material" ]
   indexOfRefraction .34
   diffuseColor .8 .54 1
```

Multiple *isA* relationships may be specified in order of preference; implementations are expected to use the first relationship mentioned for which there is a corresponding definition. *isa* relationships provide a valuable technique for extending the definitions of existing node types to add special properties for particular uses; this is often easier than defining new node types from scratch.

Summary

In this chapter, we've looked at the VRML nodes used to create scenes, and to provide them with their textures, light sources, and levels of detail. At this point, these description tools may seem a little abstract. But understanding these tools is the key to building workable virtual realities, so they're definitely worth getting to know. That's why we recommend that you not only examine our descriptions of VRML in this book, but that you also spend time with the VRML specification itself. Its URL, as we mentioned in Chapter 1, is:

```
http://vrml.wired.com/vrml.tech/vrml10-3.html
```

In the next chapter, we'll change focus to examine some of the options available for viewing VRML worlds and scenes, as we talk about scene description standards and toolkits, and about the many varieties of VRML viewers available on the Internet today.

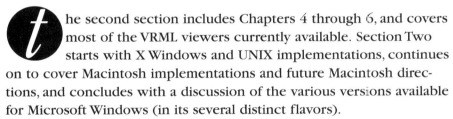

Section

Two

Viewing VRML

he second section includes Chapters 4 through 6, and covers most of the VRML viewers currently available. Section Two starts with X Windows and UNIX implementations, continues on to cover Macintosh implementations and future Macintosh directions, and concludes with a discussion of the various versions available for Microsoft Windows (in its several distinct flavors).

In Chapter 4, "X Window System Viewers," you'll learn about the various X Windows VRML viewers, including those built for high-speed, high-powered proprietary graphical workstations like those from SGI. You'll also learn about software written for more generic UNIX varieties like BSD, SCO, Linux, and Solaris. Because UNIX is the traditional home of Internet- and Web-focused development, it should come as no surprise that these viewers offer some of the most powerful and sophisticated VRML capabilities we've seen anywhere, and clearly lead the pack in power, capability, and price.

In Chapter 5, "VRML on the Mac," you'll learn about the current dearth of Macintosh VRML viewers and some of the reasons why this may not be the case for too much longer. You'll take an in-depth look at Whurlwind, the only native Macintosh VRML viewer available as we were writing this book, and some of its not inconsiderable capabilities.

Chapter 6, "The VRML Windows Browsers," is the final chapter of Section Two. Here, you'll be exposed to several of the interesting varieties of VRML viewers available for Windows NT, Windows 95 (and some even for Windows 3.1, 3.11, or Windows for Workgroups). These include VRWeb for Windows, developed by a consortium composed of IICM, NCSA, and the Gopher team from the University of Minnesota; WebSpace, the product of an alliance between SGI and Template Graphics Software; and WorldView for Windows, designed and developed by InterVista Software. Along the way, you'll learn about capabilities, performance, and pros and cons of the various packages.

At the end of this section of the book, you should understand what kinds of VRML viewers are available on the various platforms, and be able to appreciate their varying capabilities, strengths, and weaknesses.

## CHAPTER 4

X Window System
Viewers

t oday, the best available VRML viewers are UNIX-based applications created by SGI. These viewers can rely either on specific hardware, like a snazzy graphics accelerator, or on one of the OpenGL library variants, discussed later in this chapter.

Although originally developed for UNIX workstations, there has been a renewed focus on the creation of smaller, tighter VRML viewers that can run on a modestly equipped microcomputer much like the ones that many people have at the office or at home. This represents a significantly expanded market for VRML technology than earlier implementations could allow.

These nascent VRML browsers were built on UNIX systems because of the wide selection of graphics libraries available for the rapid prototyping of graphics-intensive software. Building on the work of others who created image rendering and object-oriented modeling software, VRML's original goals were to get up and running as quickly as possible. What made this possible was the inclusion of already developed file formats and code libraries with the appropriate hooks for further elaboration. In this chapter, you'll see this at work, as we discuss the different mechanisms for using and obtaining VRML viewers to operate on your X Windows workstation.

The most capable VRML viewers, by far, are those written specifically for the SGI platform. Silicon Graphics has played a major role in VRML's definition and specifications, and some of the principles applied in the VRML design use parts borrowed mainly from SGI's Open Inventor and OpenGL toolsets. This explains the relative abundance of SGI-based VRML applications and the concomitant lack of microcomputer VRML implementations.

The first half of this chapter deals with the varieties of alphabet soup you might encounter as you try to configure and set up your VRML viewer. The second half of this chapter describes our experiences in setting up the few viewers that we could obtain. It also describes our adventures in determining what we could actually get running, given our available selection of equipment. Unfortunately, the best of the VRML systems were all SGI-based implementations; since we lacked access to any SGI equipment, we chose a few of the more generic X Windows-based implementations widely available on the Internet.

Our Set Up, Plus Minimal Requirements

Given the computation and graphics-intensive nature of X Windows and VRML, a nearly ideal platform would be a Sparc 20 with 128MB RAM and a 9GB hard drive, with a T3 connection. Given that such systems are out of reach for ordinary mortals, we put together a list of the minimal hardware configuration suitable for running VRML applications. We hasten to qualify these guidelines by adding that this list is provided as a simple statement of minimal requirements; it's not intended to supply purchasing guidelines, nor to recommend any specific pieces of equipment.

- X11-R4 or later (we had the best luck with X11-R5).
- 32MB RAM.
- 256-color video display (we were able to get a 16- color version running, but it looked hideous).
- 28.8Kbps connection to the Internet. Although most of our tests were conducted on a T1 backbone to the Internet, we were able to make a 28.8 modem work with a modicum of success.

We used a Sun Sparc 2 (running SunOS 4.1.3), a Sun Sparc 20 (running Solaris 5.3), a 486 DX4/100 PC (running LINUX), and an IBM RS/6000 for our testing. Unfortunately, we had no access to an SGI machine, which we dearly missed, because most of the really interesting VRML applications are still specific to that platform.

OpenGL and Its Libraries

Our discussion begins with a more detailed examination of the
OpenGL suite, which is a software interface for designing graphical
applications that can generate both 2-D and 3-D graphics. OpenGL was
constructed with the idea of an open architecture in mind (hence its
name); consequently, it is deliberately operating- and windowing-system
independent.

More important, OpenGL's creators deemed it necessary to also keep
it unhinged from any native hardware, which is where its greatest
advantages shine forth. As a result, many popular vendors have adopted
the OpenGL libraries and incorporated them into their architecture.
This not only makes life easier for graphics programmers, it also lends
itself to laying higher-level groundwork for cross-platform, hardware-
independent languages like VRML.

Specifically...

OpenGL comes equipped with a vast selection of graphics primitives
and functions, including everything from depositing a single point, to
generating a realistic model of a C130 airplane from a model comprised
of a million tiny polygons. Furthermore, OpenGL supports adding texture maps to objects defined in its environment, and can handle curved
surfaces with ease. Given this kind of resume, it explains why the triumvirate of Bell, Parisi, and Pesci chose a toolkit based on OpenGL for
their initial implementation of VRML.

Taken from the OpenGL FAQ, the following list names all of the
major componentry and functionality that makes OpenGL such a great
graphics development library:

```
Geometric primitives (points, lines, and polygons)
Raster primitives (bitmaps and pixel rectangles)
RGBA or color index mode
Display list or immediate mode
Viewing and modeling transformations
Hidden Surface Removal (depth buffer)
Alpha Blending (transparency)
Antialiasing
Texture Mapping
Atmospheric Effects (fog, smoke, and haze)
```

```
Polynomial Evaluators (to support Non-uniform rational B-splines)
Pixel Operations (storing, transforming, mapping, zooming)
Accumulation Buffer
Stencil Planes
Feedback, Selection, and Picking
```

As we mentioned earlier, OpenGL's most important aspect is its portability. By using an implementation that works regardless of hardware and operating system, applications built around OpenGL can serve more users.

Here's another crucial snippet, straight from the OpenGL FAQ:

OpenGL is the software interface for graphics hardware that allows graphics programmers to produce high-quality color images of 3-D objects. OpenGL is a rendering only, vendor neutral API providing 2-D and 3-D graphics functions, including modeling, transformations, color, lighting, smooth shading, as well as advanced features like texture mapping, NURBS, fog, alpha blending and motion blur. OpenGL works in both immediate and retained (display list) graphics modes. OpenGL is window system and operating system independent. OpenGL has been integrated with Windows NT and with the X Window System under UNIX. Also, OpenGL is network transparent. A defined common extension to the X Window System allows an OpenGL client on one vendor's platform to run across a network to another vendor's OpenGL server.

The key ingredients to remember are the power and richness of the graphical operations supported, and the independence from particular windowing or operating systems (evidenced further by references to multiple implementations and the ease of networked access). For access to the FAQ, please consult this URL:

```
http://www.cis.ohio-
state.edu/hypertext/faq/bngusenet/comp/graphics/opengl/top.html
```

How is the OpenGL standard maintained?

Like most standards, OpenGL is governed by an independent board. Its controlling body is known as the *Architecture Review Board* (ARB). Each ARB member has one vote about where the OpenGL standard is going, and what options should be included in its future incarnations.

The permanent members of the ARB include companies like DEC, IBM, Intel, Microsoft, and SGI. As things unfold in the VRML arena, we are sure to see some new additions to the board, probably from startup companies currently working either on VRML browsers or on basic VRML language implementations.

Some OpenGL Web sites for more information

These three sites offer a variety of information on VRML, including sites and viewpoints taken from industry and academia:

```
http://hertz.eng.ohio-state.edu/~hts/opengl/article.html
http://www.sgi.com/Technology/openGL/
http://www.sd.tgs.com/~template/Products/opengl.html
```

GLUT (Graphics Library Utility Toolkit)

If you are interested in developing graphics libraries or just like to keep tabs on what is going on within that realm, GLUT is worth checking out. It's a portable toolkit designed to interoperate with OpenGL. The GLUT 2.0 version supports a literal cornucopia of goodies including multiple windows for OpenGL renderers, callback-driven event processing, advanced input widgets like dials and buttons, idle loops, timers, popup menus, solid object shortcuts, bitmap inclusions, and finally, access to the OpenGL extension query system.

The source code and specification, as well as articles about GLUT, can be found at the GLUT ftp site:

```
ftp://sgigate.sgi.com/pub/opengl/xjournal/GLUT
```

GLUT 2.0 has been tested on the following platforms:

• DEC Alpha workstations running OSF/1 with the Open3D layered product

• IBM RS/6000 workstations running AIX with OpenGL support

• SGI workstations running IRIX 5.2 (or higher) that support OpenGL

• Template Graphics Software's OpenGL for Sun workstations

• Mesa 1.1 for UNIX workstations

GLUT can be downloaded from SGI's Web site at:

```
http://www.sgi.com/Technology/openGL/glut.html
```

Open Inventor (the Next Level Up)

Open Inventor, as we mentioned in Chapter 1, is a 3-D toolkit that also defines a rich set of graphics utilities. However, the most compelling reason for including it here is that it defines a common interchange file format for 3-D graphics and rendering. You can think of the Inventor File Format (IFF) as akin to the "Rich Text Format" employed by such companies as Microsoft. That is, it uses a common set of marked-up text tags to specify formatting clues so that one program may exchange its data with a similar program running on a different platform, or even a different application altogether.

In the same vein, any VRML viewer can read a scene file produced by another application, as long as it adheres to the IFF. Even though the scene may have been produced on a different machine, possibly for a different purpose, it remains viewable. By using a generic file format, VRML ensures itself longevity as a rendering language.

Since Open Inventor is a toolkit for specifying 3-D scenes, it is naturally object-oriented. Each object (or node) is defined to scope the various properties that need to be included within it, separated by other objects or specialized separator fields. As mentioned in the specifics of the VRML language in Chapters 2 and 3, VRML's linearity is important to its overall structure. The Open Inventor file format, by giving the scene designer the power to manipulate multiple distinct objects in linear fashion, was chosen because of this orderly behavior, along with its portability.

Another of Open Inventor's bonuses is that it comes replete with a collection of primitives intended for designing 3-D scenes. Its supply of simple cubes and other polyhedral objects, and of cameras, light sources, and other materials is quite comprehensive.

As a final point in praise of Open Inventor, this toolkit includes numerous usable predefined solutions for interactive programming problems. By providing developers with simple interfaces to movement and vectors, as well as perspective cues, Inventor meets some of VRML's most serious requirements—namely, that it be extensible, and that it allow a wide range of interactivity and movement when the time comes to develop such a mechanism.

Although IFF is the de facto standard for 3-D manipulation on the Silicon Graphics architecture, its recent inclusion in other systems and the fact that it is the basis for some other graphics work (like VRML) has made it a likely candidate for a common standard for any machine.

For more information about Open Inventor, look at the FAQ:

```
http://www.sgi.com/Technology/Inventor/FAQ.html
```

Mesa

Since OpenGL and Open Inventor are both specific to the SGI platform, the need for a generic X Window System-based graphics library that supported all of their implementation aspects and perks soon made itself felt in the rest of the UNIX community. Thankfully, such a library was developed by Brian Paul of the Space Science and Engineering Center at the University of Wisconsin at Madison. His library, called Mesa, does an exemplary job of providing an OpenGL-like API for use when Inventor is not available (as in our case).

Even though an exact duplicate of OpenGL would ruffle SGI's feathers, Mesa's author merely states that the relevant parts of Mesa are used with SGI's authority. Further, he makes no claims as to Mesa's replacement value for OpenGL overall.

Mesa is distributed under the terms of the GNU Library Public License. All parties interested in obtaining a fully-licensed OpenGL implementation should consult an appropriate vendor.

What is GPL?

The GNU General Public License (GPL) was proposed by Richard Stallman of the Free Software Foundation to encourage the development of important software without the traditional barriers that encumber products getting to market, or that stifle their development once they are in an established market.

A piece of software that is declared by its author to be under the GPL is said to be *copylefted*, as opposed to *copyrighted*. Whenever a copylefted product is distributed, its source code must be available as well, so that any user can alter, recompile, and reconfigure it ad infinitum. But any changes, fixes, or upgrades that are made to that source code must be placed back in the original product, with the source code of the new contribution. Thus the product continues to improve without being held by a single individual or company.

Further, any individual or company can package and sell products that are under GPL, but they must still make the source code to the product available. Anyone who buys the product is free to recopy, alter, or redistribute the product so long as the GPL is followed.

Presently, Mesa runs on most of the X environments available for "stock" UNIX systems on most platforms. Mesa has also been ported to Microsoft Windows, and implementations for the Macintosh and MS DOS are underway as of this writing. Since Mesa doesn't rely on performance supplied by specific hardware (like superfast graphics cards), its performance is a direct function of CPU and X Window System speeds and feeds.

The following features are fully implemented:

```
all point, line and polygon primitives
all model and view transformations
lighting
smooth shading
depth buffering
clipping (against user clip planes and view volume)
accumulation buffer
alpha testing/blending
stencil buffer
dithering
logic operations
evaluators (curves and surfaces)
feedback/selection
fog/depth cueing
polygon/line stippling
read/write/copy pixels
tk and aux libraries for X11
context switching (multiple windows)
RGB mode simulated in color mapped windows
Support for Mark Kilgard's GLUT
SGI's blending extensions
```

The following features are mostly or partially implemented:

```
display lists (~90% complete)
texture mapping (~50% complete)
the GLU utility library
a set of pseudo-GLX functions
```

The following features aren't implemented at all:

```
antialiasing
glPixelZoom
NURBS
```

Despite its partial or incomplete implementations and its outright deficiencies (compared to OpenGL), Mesa offers significant capabilities and promises to make VRML implementation easier on a wide variety of computing platforms.

Where to get Mesa

Mesa is available by anonymous ftp at:

```
ftp://iris.ssec.wisc.edu/pub/Mesa/Mesa-1.2.1.tar.Z
```

Our goal here is to illustrate that many (if not most) of the other plat-forms that will ultimately support VRML may be using the Mesa libraries directly, or some future variant of Mesa. We also stress that although Mesa and Inventor are very similar, they are still not equal, and the future of VRML implementations will probably see OpenGL-based viewers on the high-function, high-cost side of the market, and Mesa-based viewers on the lower-function, lower-cost side.

VRML Viewers for X

With that caveat about OpenGL and Mesa in mind, let's explore the X Windows VRML scene and the available viewers. Along the way, you'll meet some pretty interesting software!

Getting your X Web browser to call it

Although we used Netscape for the bulk of our testing, the setups for a Mosaic and CERN system are similar if not exactly the same, as we'll describe later. In Figure 4-1 you'll notice the standard Netscape Preferences dialog box has been preset to the "Helper Application" section; this is no coincidence, because when it comes to viewing VRML, it's the section that concerns us the most.

Our first goal is to instruct your Web browser about what to do with VRML files as they come knocking at your door. This requires that you modify the Preferences file for your browser to enable it to accept a new MIME type—namely, "x-world/x-vrml". You'll also need to tell the browser what the default extension for files of this type will be; for VRML, this is most commonly ".WRL", but we have seen ".VRML" used in rare instances.

We recommend that you change the application defaults. rather than ones stored in your home directory, unless your access won't permit this (i.e., for Netscape, you'd change the "/usr/local/lib/netscape/ .mime.types" file rather than your own personal "~/.mime.types" file).

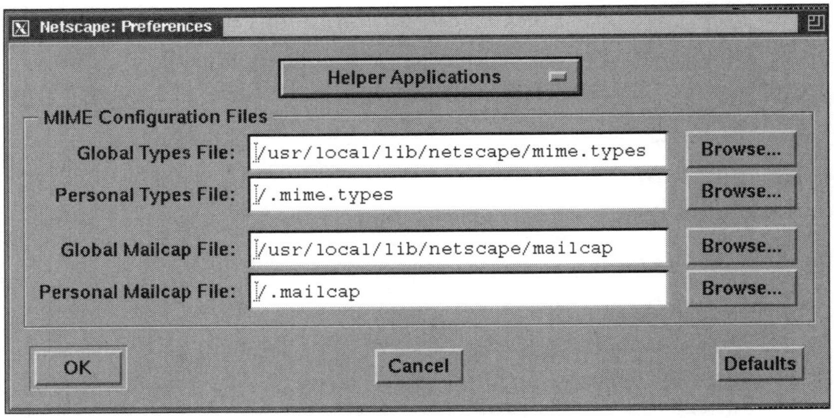

Figure 4-1: Netscape's X Preferences dialog box.

To make this kind of change, you may have to coordinate with your system administrator.

In our tests, we used both Netscape for X and XMosaic. We were easily able to modify them so that when we encountered a VRML file ("*.WRL") on the Web, we were able to successfully download and view its corresponding scene.

Let's look at how this works: A parallel operation is executed when retrieving a sound, or when downloading a gzipped file ("*.gz"). Before the Web server sends any data, it explains what it is going to send by indicating an appropriate MIME type. It gets its MIME type information from the extension to the file that it is about to send.

In the case of VRML files, any file ending with ".WRL" is considered a VRML file with a MIME type of "x-world/x-vrml". An analogous action takes place on the receiving end when your browser gets handed the file. First, the MIME type sent is checked against a registry of known types, stored in the ".mime.types" file. If a corresponding entry is found, the associated application is then executed treating the file just received as its first argument. In short, this "pass-the-buck" system is in use by all browsers on any machine running any OS.

Here are some steps that were necessary to get our MIME types file properly configured, and what you can do with your browser once the VRML helper application has been successfully integrated.

1. Edit your ".mime.types" file and add the following line:

```
x-world/x-vrml  wrl
```

74

2. Edit your ".mailcap" and add the following line:

```
x-world/x-vrml; /install_directory/vrweb %s;
```

When you add the actual line, please replace the string "install_directory" with the absolute path for your vrweb installation directory.

These instructions may be used for any VRML viewer that you intend to install. You'll need to change the "install_directory" as well as the "vrweb" designation to reflect whatever application you want to launch. You might also need to have root privileges in order to modify these files on your system. If you are using an xterminal connected to an X workstation, you might also try modifying your specific ".mailcap" and ".mime.types" files, which are usually located in your home directory.

Be careful of world (".WRL") files that are compressed at the server end. Since VRML scene files can get quite large, sometimes Web administrators will compress these files to conserve disk space. In that case, you'll need to tell your browser to accept "x-compressed" files as well, and you'll need to uncompress them on-the-fly before you can view them with your VRML browser. Be especially mindful of the different compression techniques in use, and make preference changes to reflect at least the major options, including ".GZ", ".ZIP", and the most likely "*.Z".

VRWeb for X

VRWeb is one of the few current VRML browsers that supports several operating systems in its infancy, and has proved to be quite a good resource in our exploration of the language.

Background of the VRWeb project

The VRWeb undertaking began in April, 1995 as a joint work in progress comprised of IICM (the Hyper-G Team), NCSA, and lastly the Gopher team. (Further discussion of the parties that created VRWeb can be found in Chapter 6 under the heading: VRWeb for Windows.)

VRWeb for X utilizes the Mesa graphics toolkit. Because there is only sparse documentation available with the package, we can't provide you with any text clips from the creators to describe its exact use. The reason for this lack of documentation is that VRWeb is a virgin product barely out of its infancy. Even though it already runs on several platforms, we've learned that "real documentation" is usually created at the end of a project's development cycle. We therefore look forward to some good stuff from these guys, if VRWeb is any indication of their potential.

How to use VRWeb for X

The VRWeb browser is based on the Harmony scene viewer that is part of Hyper-G. In Figure 4-2 we show off VRWeb's interface by using it to open a sample VRML file that we retrieved from the Internet. As you can see, the rendering engine behind VRWeb makes quite a nice picture.

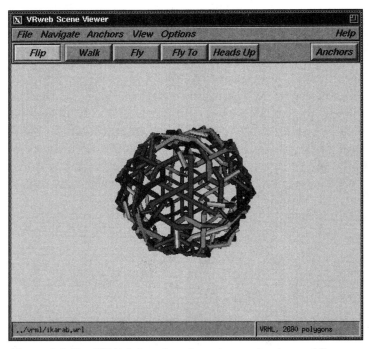

Figure 4-2: The VRWeb interface in action, a nice knot, eh?

Much of the action involved in getting VRWeb to operate is handled by the menu bar, rather than by the navigation buttons found at the top of the window. Other than the standard items found in the File menu, there isn't much noteworthy here. The View menu allows you to access items found in the button area, but we consider this rather superfluous in its present state.

The Rendering menu item gives you control over the level of detail at which you would like your scene to be displayed. Options range from wireframe diagrams to smooth, polished drawings. Of course, the better you want something to look, the longer you have to wait to get it (an axiom for life in general, we would suppose).

The rendering level you actually need depends on the speed and precision of the 3-D model that you're viewing. If you are sketching out a simple frame, to be flushed out and modeled in greater detail later, you would obviously only need to use the wireframe option, which also displays the fastest. A look at a wireframe model of the picture we presented in Figure 4-2 is presented in Figure 4-3 below. Notice how much easier it is to render, and thus quicker to display, but also how crude it is.

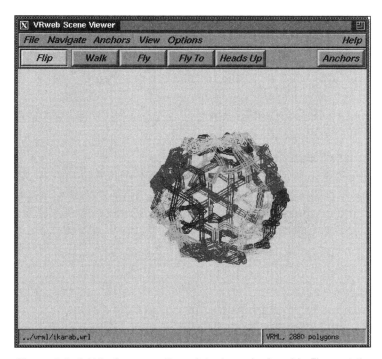

Figure 4-3: A Wireframe outline of the knot depicted in Figure 4-2.

By using the Navigation menu, you can interact with your virtual world in a multitude of ways. The Fly mode allows you to move about by dragging the mouse over different areas of the screen. As an added bonus, a different response may be achieved by holding down each of the various mouse buttons, as an action is requested. By clicking on the Flip button, for instance, the status bar at the bottom of the screen presents the following options:"Drag mouse to translate/rotate/zoom the model." Each of these three options is mapped to the three mouse buttons. By pressing the middle mouse button and dragging from one edge of the image to the center, a 90 degree rotation is elicited.

The same applies to the Walk button, which gives you the option to "walk/move/look." While in the Walk mode, you are allowed to move around the world as if you were walking: you can go forward, backward, left, or right, but not up or down.

The final Navigation selection is the Heads Up display, which is a sort of quick jumping-off point for each of the other options. It is a collection of four icons that appears over your image; it allows you to quickly perform the step represented by the icon. The top icon lets you fly around the scene; the second lets you walk; the third icon, which resembles a set of compass arrows, lets you move the camera along the x- or y-axis; the bottom icon zooms to the area targeted by the crosshairs. In Figure 4-4, we've taken a snapshot of our X Window System with a picture of a multisided polygon, with the Heads Up controls painted over the middle.

Where to find VRWeb for X

For general release information, and for complete discussions on where the VRWeb project stands and where it is going, please start at the following page for the most up-to-date announcements (WARNING: you'll have to do some rooting around to get to the VRWeb page from here, but given the "ugly" nature of its specific URL, we chose this URL instead):

```
http://hgiicm.tu-graz.ac.at/
```

Although many of our tests were conducted using a SUN Sparc 2 with 32MB RAM, we did notice that a fair amount of time was needed for normal image rendering, which typically took from 2 to 20 seconds (for 100 to 10,000 polygons of varying degrees of complexity). It should be noted, however, that as we're writing this book, VRWeb is still in its infancy and perforce, our tests used beta versions. We can expect significant performance increases as the final product becomes available some time within the next year.

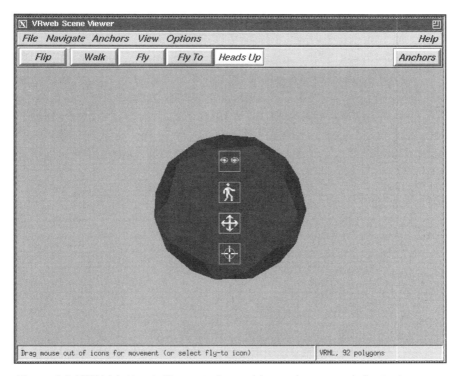

Figure 4-4: VRWeb's Heads Up controls provide good command shortcuts.

WebSpace, Tested Using the Solaris Version

Since it seems that all roads in VRML lead back to SGI, it is only natural, that SGI has its own Web-based VRML viewer under development. Based on the Open Inventor format around which VRML was originally built, SGI offers their VRML browser as a part of their Web authoring hardware/software solution.

Dubbed WebSpace, the VRML browser makes up part of their overall Web server solution, billed as the SGI WebFORCE package. To get more information about what platforms WebSpace supports, as well as timely reports on SGI's development activity, check out this URL:

```
http://www.sgi.com/Products/WebFORCE/WebSpace/
```

Although WebSpace is just another X Windows application, much like VRWeb in its capabilities and performance, it was very different in its platform and requirements. Here's a complete list of what we minimally needed to get it running on our Sun:

- A ZX (aka "Leo") or TZX 3-D graphics accelerator
- Solaris 2.3 or 2.4 (2.4 recommended)
- Netscape 1.1 (if you wish to download VRML files from the Web)
- 8MB disk space (imposed by the developers)

Of course, this whole exercise would have been a million times easier if we had had a spare SGI box or two just lying around (which we are sad to report was *not* the case). For more information on how to get your SUN SparcStation to cooperate with WebSpace, try checking out the documentation found at SGI:

```
ftp://sgigate.sgi.com/pub/Surf/WebSpace/tgs/Sun/Readme.txt
```

Silicon Graphics is only producing WebSpace for SGI platforms and has commissioned Template Graphics Software in California to handle its development for all other platforms, including the Windows and Sun versions we've tested for this book. Information about WebSpace for X, as well as for other platforms, can be retrieved from Template's site at:

```
http://www.sd.tgs.com/~template/WebSpace/monday.html
```

No support is offered for the various beta versions unless you register them with Template Graphics for $49.00 each. But registration includes a free upgrade to the final version of WebSpace V1.0 when it is released.

We spoke with the public relations people at SGI, who were very nice indeed and forwarded us the screenshots (Figures 4-5 through 4-8) of what their browser looks like for the SGI platform itself. They also included lots of interesting product information that described their viewer, along with detailing its capabilities. (Sigh! If only we had a spare $40K or so for glamorous hardware...)

WebView

Another X Windows SGI-only application is WebView, created by Dave Nadeau, Cherilyn Michaels, John Moreland, and Dema Zlotin at the San Diego Supercomputer Center. WebView is an application that we downloaded but were unable to use without an SGI workstation, which is seemingly the only platform where this application would compile successfully.

WebView will reportedly open either a VRML file or a URL passed to it, and allow the user to manipulate the resulting image in 3-D space as well as navigate around, or interact with, the VRML scene. To accom-

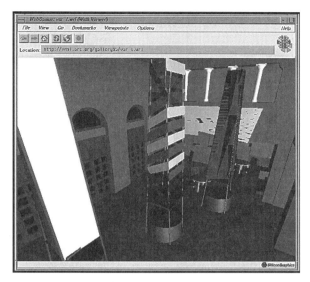

Figure 4-5: SGI's WebSpace browser showing the Arc VRML site's lobby.

plish the magic of opening up the URL, a command-line argument is generally passed to WebView preceded with a "-URL" option flag. Here's an example of this syntax:

```
WebView -URL http://vrml.abc.com/vrml_files/house_part1.wrl
```

Of course, this is a bogus URL but the point should be well illustrated. Some of the features that WebView will support includes the

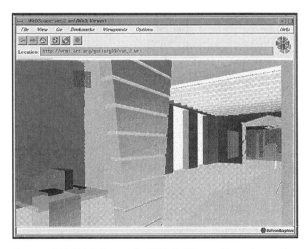

Figure 4-6: WebSpace in "Walk Viewer" mode on the second floor of the Arc site.

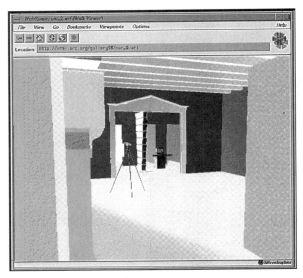

Figure 4-7: Another WebSpace "Walk Viewer" of the Arc site's 2nd floor.

ability to fully handle the entire VRML version 1.0 specification, as well as a scene-graph viewer/editor for creating and editing scenes as they are retrieved. This latter feature should prove quite advantageous in the months to come, as working with VRML becomes more commonplace.

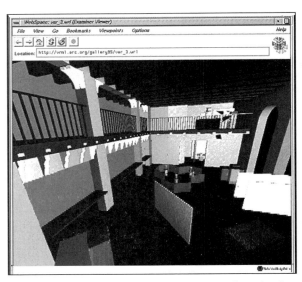

Figure 4-8: WebSpace's "Examine Viewer" mode showing off more of the Variety Arts Center.

The following are some of WebView's more powerful features:

- Permits multi-window viewing of individual environments.
- Supports all SGI Open Inventor viewers.
- Generates a Viewpoints menu containing a scene's predefined cameras.
- Provides automated disk and memory caching of scenes.
- Processes URLs so it can act as a standalone browser or as a helper application.
- Presently runs only on SGI platforms.

Given this feature set, we look forward to a day when we can use this program on our Suns or LINUX machines, as well as in the more rarefied atmosphere on SGI equipment.

Summary

In this chapter, we previewed some of the work on VRML underway in the UNIX workstation arena, specifically on X Window System machines. In addition, we visited the libraries that typically form these applications, and finished off by exploring the capabilities and requirements for three of the most common browsers. We also discussed the relevance of the Mesa library and its relation to the SGI Open Inventor format, and ventured some predictions about where these toolkits are going.

## CHAPTER 5

VRML on the Mac
The Current State of Things

having looked at the roots of VRML on UNIX running under X Windows, we now consider the Macintosh platform. We'll turn first to the playing field as a whole, for a quick survey of browser development teams and where they are going. Then we'll look at the first Mac VRML browser to hit the testing circuit and, given the dearth of Macintosh-based browsers and authoring tools at this moment, we'll discuss some future products. Finally, we'll explore some of the underlying technologies at Apple that may take the Mac from its slow start in VRML to a first place finish.

The Internet on the Mac

Despite the continuing dominance of Wintel PCs (Microsoft Windows running on an Intel platform), the Internet has been one segment of the computing world where the Macintosh family of computers holds more than its usual 10% of the market. This has its roots in the Internet's traditional user base that springs largely from the higher education market. Apple is traditionally stronger there than in consumer or business markets and enjoys a kind of overexposure on the Internet.

The ease of use of the Mac TCP/IP implementation, with the MacTCP control panel, combined with the general elegance of its user interface, has resulted in disproportionate attention to early development of Internet tools for the Mac. Primarily, these tools have been clients for Internet services delivered from UNIX-based servers.

As the Internet has graduated from college, it's become increasingly commercialized. Today, the emphasis on software development has started to take on a familiar look, adopted from the "real world" computer market. When new services spring to life—like the Internet Phone, or Real Audio—clients are developed for the Wintel platform at the same time, if not before, the Macintosh platform.

VRML on the Mac?

VRML has followed the mass market development model more closely than any services that preceded it. All the first-to-market VRML browsers run on Windows 3.1, Windows 95, or NT. WebSpace, the first of these early browsers, was originally developed by SGI and initially supported only SGI workstations. When the time came to push WebSpace out to a larger market, they called on Template Graphics Software to port version 1.0 to Solaris, IBM AIX, Windows 3.1, and Windows NT. In their own words, "follow-on WebSpace releases will support the Macintosh and other miscellaneous platforms."

Worldview, developed by one of VRML's originators, Tony Parisi, was actually the first-to-market Windows 3.1 browser. His company, Intervista, has announced plans to support the Macintosh by September, 1995. But even as late as the summer of 1995, we were unable to obtain any running code from Intervista, nor any updated timetable for their Mac release.

VRWeb's pedigree, springing as it does from the people who brought us Telnet, Gopher, and Mosaic, might lead you to suppose that a Macintosh version would be available soon. However, neither NCSA nor the University of Minnesota has made any mention of VRWeb for the Macintosh, either in development or planning stages. Perhaps this isn't quite as surprising as it might appear since VRWeb depends largely on the Mesa 3D graphics library. Mesa was developed on UNIX and has only recently been ported to DOS/Windows. Furthermore, this consortium's VRML development efforts are spearheaded by IICM, an almost exclusively UNIX/DOS/Windows development operation.

With Apple's adoption of the PowerPC chip family and the development of several key graphics technologies, the Macintosh is better suited than ever for VRML. The raw horsepower of the PPC chips compares favorably to the fastest Pentium machines and even to UNIX workstations of the kind where VRML browsers were first prototyped.

Thankfully, the always plucky Macintosh developer community is stepping in to save the day, both inside and outside of Apple. A flurry of recent activity should lead to the rapid development of VRML browsers and authoring tools that may end up being the best in their class!

Home, Home on a 2-D Plane

The first working Macintosh VRML browser is an application called Whurlwind, written by William Enright and Jon Louch. Tested in a raw, pre-alpha state, Whurlwind proved to be a superb performer, when run using the following configuration:

- Apple Power Macintosh 6100/60Mhz
- 16Mb RAM, 16Mb virtual memory
- 350Mb SCSI hard drive
- AV card w/2Mb VRAM
- Apple 15" Multiple Scan monitor
- Microcom v.34 Deskporte EP 28.8Kbps modem, connecting to an Internet Service Provider with 1.544Mbs T1 link
- System 7.5, System Update 1.0
- QuickDraw 3D 1.0

Whurlwind is best described as an elegant hack and we mean that in the most complimentary way possible. The programmers grabbed QvLib shortly after it was made public by SGI, in the spring of 1995, and ported it to the Macintosh. QvLib is, of course, the parser library that takes VRML code and wrestles it into a form that Macintosh developers can use in their programs.

After building QvLib, Enright and Louch then translated its parsed output into the newly available QuickDraw 3D code libraries and viewer. Voila! Instant VRML browser—and smoking hot, at that!

QuickDraw 3D—The Latest Twist to the MacOS

In Summer 1995, Apple made available to developers pre-release versions of QuickDraw 3D extensions to the MacOS. Then, in an unprecedented move, the product team decided to make the developers' nascent efforts available to the public through the World Wide Web. The URL for the QuickDraw 3D site is:

```
http://www.info.apple.com/qd3d/QD3D.HTML
```

They hoped to create a buzz and groundswell of support making QuickDraw 3D the cross-platform standard for 3-D objects and scenes, providing developers with a reliable API.

QuickDraw 3D offers a high-level modeling toolkit, cross-platform file format, and robust human interface guidelines. On the device level it has built-in management for input devices and hardware acceleration. Combined, these features make QuickDraw 3D very attractive to the cross-platform developer.

If Apple is successful and QuickDraw 3D is widely adopted across the industry, it could herald a new era of high-end modeling and rendering applications readily available to consumers. Much like QuickTime, QuickDraw 3D has the potential to open up vast markets to developers, which should spur them to bring new products to market.

It's also noteworthy that QuickDraw 3D represents the first software technology developed by Apple exclusively for the PowerPC. This was a decision based on performance considerations, where only a RISC architecture could deliver the raw horsepower required for the job.

There are some caveats we must offer regarding Whurlwind. First, its dependence upon QuickDraw 3D means that it requires a PowerPC platform. Also, in its current pre-release state, Whurlwind can't open a large percentage of existing ".wrl" files. The programmers are actively chasing bugs, so we feel confident Whurlwind will be functioning properly by the time you read this.

In the same vein, the pre-release Whurlwind is somewhat lean on features, with barebones but adequate navigation. WWW in-line graphics and anchors aren't supported, nor have textures been implemented. Obviously the Whurlwind team has a long way to go before their viewer holds its own in every aspect of design, features, and performance. Nevertheless, we're impressed with what we've seen so far!

The Interface—Minimal, but Good

With these caveats in mind, let's take a look at the software. The first thing you'll notice is that Whurlwind is designed as a helper application, not a standalone Web browser. Therefore, it requires a browser like Netscape, Mosaic, or MacWeb that can be configured with the "x-world/x-vrml" MIME type as described in Chapter 6. (One quick-note: please make sure, when creating your MIME definitions, to map both "wrl" and "vrml" to the "x-world/x-vrml" type. There's still a mixture of both floating around on the Net.)

Whurlwind requires the QuickDraw 3D 1.0 extension and the QuickDraw 3D Acceleration and Viewer shared libraries. As mentioned, this dependency on QuickDraw 3D means that Whurlwind only runs on PowerPCs, and in all likelihood will never run on a 680x0 Mac. This is not necessarily bad, since the horsepower provided by the PowerPC is what makes this browser so usable.

Whurlwind has a default memory allocation of 2,000K but as with everything graphical, and especially three-dimensional, you can never really have enough RAM. We doubled its allocation to 4,000K and were able to open three or four decent-sized scenes at a time. This highlights a crucial difference between Whurlwind and the Windows browsers—namely, Whurlwind's ability to open multiple VRML files at one time.

As for actual files, Whurlwind does quite well with the majority of the basic shape and solid files we found at the VRML archive at:

```
ftp://ftp.vrml.org/
```

in the "pub/GoodModels" directory. This includes everything from the simple spheres to complex compound shapes.

Our first look at a Whurlwind document window (see Figures 5-1 and 5-2) illustrates the application's minimalist interface. For now, the developers rely solely on the default interface provided with the basic QuickDraw 3D viewer. There are four buttons presented along the bottom edge of the window: from left to right, these are the *camera* selector, *distance* tool, *rotation* tool, and *panning* tool.

The camera selector, presents a popup menu of the viewpoints available in a particular scene. There is also a Custom Camera choice that we presume will allow users to specify new viewpoints in a future implementation. For now, selecting any Camera returns you to the starting point for the scene.

Figure 5-1: A simple solid displayed by Whurlwind.

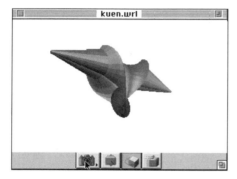

Figure 5-2: Whurlwind displays a complex geometric shape, a file named "kuen.wrl".

The distance tool lets you zoom in and out on an image by clicking the mouse and moving the cursor up or down on the document window. This has the effect of increasing and decreasing the z-value of your coordinates. Similarly, the panning tool affects the x and y coordinates, moving an object up, down, left, or right with a simple click and drag.

The rotation tool lets you influence a scene by clicking and dragging with your mouse. Using an exceedingly simple interface paradigm, the rotation tool allows you to rotate a scene to a new orientation. When you select a scene with this tool, a circular wireframe appears around its center; then, dragging the cursor rotates the model around the axes nearest to the point of selection.

This elegant design makes the controls feel natural and simulates the feeling of physically grabbing an object and spinning it around. The only drawback is the lack of precise controls over the point being rotated. This sometimes makes it difficult to achieve the desired effects.

As a basic part of the QuickDraw 3D viewer interface, we found the rotation tool to be excellent.

One interesting side effect of working so intimately with QuickDraw 3D's infrastructure is that Whurlwind is able to open files in the native QuickDraw 3D format, 3DMF (3D Meta-File), just as easily as it can open VRML files (see Figure 5-3).

Figure 5-3: A 3DMF file displayed by Whurlwind.

Whurlwind's ease of access and use speaks to the flexibility and robustness of the QuickDraw 3D libraries and interface. This may even have some interesting ramifications as other applications adopt support for QuickDraw 3D—we may see a whole realm of opportunities offered by translation and interoperability between 3DMF and VRML.

Whurlwind also inherits its ability to drag and drop as a result of its reliance on QuickDraw 3D. If you click inside a Whurlwind window and drag the contents to the desktop, the window contents "detach" from the window itself and when released on the desktop, a *clipping file* is created. This is a bitmapped PICT file, a "snapshot," if you will, of the file as it appeared when dragged to the desktop.

While this behavior can be useful, it can also become an annoyance when you aren't deliberately trying to create a clipping file. If you just want to rotate or translate an image and the cursor sneaks outside the window, you'll wind up with a clipping file on your desktop, whether you want one or not! But since drag and drop is supported with all three of the available tools (i.e., distance, rotation, and panning), there is no difference between modifying the view of a scene and creating a clipping file. It's just something you have to get used to.

Real-World Performance

How is Whurlwind's performance for larger scenes? After all, we can't expect the Web user community to get excited about adopting a new standard if all they can do is download files that contain single objects. A typical VRML file accessible through the Web will likely include at least the contents of a single room, if not a larger, more complex scene.

At the time we tested Whurlwind, the program still suffered from some known memory allocation issues with larger *meshes*, (the QuickDraw 3D term for scenes). Even so, we were able to find a number of larger scenes that opened just fine in Whurlwind. To our delight, its performance did not seem to be affected by the size of the scene. The rotation, panning, and distance tools still responded rapidly and moved the objects smoothly, even on the largest files we viewed.

The Virtual Soma scene graph from Planet 9 Productions and Intervista opened and displayed themselves in just a few seconds (see Figure 5-4). When we repositioned these scenes, there was no noticeable delay while they were reoriented and re-rendered.

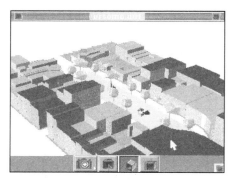

Figure 5-4: Virtual SOMA rendered by Whurlwind.

When we compare Virtual SOMA on Whurlwind to the same scene displayed by Worldview for Windows, we can see that, even in its embryonic state, Whurlwind holds its own in terms of the way it displays a scene (see Figure 5-5).

Suffice it to say that given the features and functions currently implemented in Whurlwind, its performance and interface are top-notch and we look forward to future developments with great anticipation!

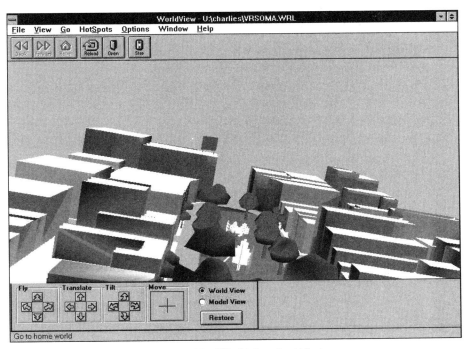

Figure 5-5: Virtual SOMA displayed by Worldview for Windows.

VRML Viewers Versus the Specification

In testing Whurlwind and other VRML browsers, we encountered numerous difficulties. Some were typical problems for code in early stages of development. Others appear provoked by inconsistencies between the way VRML files are currently authored versus how VRML is parsed in the real world.

For Whurlwind, it was immediately apparent that some files contained scenes large enough to uncover a crashing bug in its current memory allocation routines. This is the kind of thing you expect in alpha code, and it is normally fixed during the program's revision and debugging phases.

More perplexing, large numbers of smaller files would open but would only display a blank, white window. At first we wrote this phenomenon off as the result of flaky code, but over time, we noticed two things that caused us to revise our opinions:

1. Similar behavior was exhibited in all of the browsers we tested, on all the various platforms (in most other cases, the window

would be black instead of white, but blank and featureless nonetheless).

2. Despite its size and complexity, the Virtual SOMA file rendered beautifully on all the browsers we tested, without fail.

Because Tony Parisi, a co-author of the 1.0 specification, was also the creator of the Virtual SOMA site, this gave us pause. We began to believe that there might be something about the ways in which others were writing VRML scenes, compared to Parisi's no doubt well-informed techniques, that was eliciting this kind of behavior. That's what prompted further investigation and we'll share what we learned.

One interesting aspect of this behavior was that the viewers acted as if these scenes had loaded successfully. Their elements and perspectives could be manipulated using the various tools available, but the results just weren't visible. Acting on a hunch that light sources might be a culprit, we started poking around in the Virtual SOMA file to see what was different about this particular file.

Two elements immediately became apparent. First, the Virtual SOMA scene was represented in a file called "vrsoma.wrl" that wrapped all its code within a single Separator node. This is the proper way to author VRML, since the Specification states that an entire scene must be a *single* node.

The files that failed to display invariably failed to wrap their scenes in a single Separator, and were therefore comprised of a whole series of separate nodes. Interestingly, WebSpace (from TGS and SGI) seemed not to care whether a scene was a single node or not, which speaks either to its ability to read Open Inventor files or to a more intelligent level of error correction.

We located a second potential culprit when we noticed that the file Tony Parisi used to create Virtual SOMA defined each light source explicitly, without relying on a node's default values. In other words, in "vrsoma.wrl" a PointLight node was defined as:

```
PointLight {
on TRUE
intensity 1.0
color 1.0 1.0 1.0
location 0 250 1000
}
```

According to the 1.0 specification, only the "location" field needs to be explicitly defined, since other fields use their defaults. But by contrast, the files that don't render properly often define their PointLight elements like this:

```
PointLight {}
```

This assumes that all the default values will be filled in when the scene is parsed. But in several cases when a PointLight's instance was modified to mirror the way the same node appeared in "vrsoma.wrl", the scene would magically appear in our viewers!

Based on our detective work, it seems there's an error occurring somewhere during the scene traversal and parsing stage, where default values aren't filled out properly for VRML nodes. Since QvLib is the common parsing engine across all the viewers that seemed to have this problem, it appears that QvLib, alas, is the most likely culprit.

We expect that this glitch will be worked out as the development of the VRML language, its parsers, and its viewers goes forward. In fact, the example we've just described may be moot by the time you read this. Nevertheless, we hope our description will help describe the types of investigation and tweaking you may find necessary in your own adventures with VRML.

We must say that it's quite a luxury to dive right into the meat of a rendered scene and sort through its code manually. The level of control that VRML offers is not likely to be found in any other worlds, computer-generated or otherwise.

Whurlwind Development Directions

Writing a chapter on Whurlwind is a little like herding cats. We're particularly fond of this viewer but it has been a real challenge to get it to stand still long enough to run it through its paces. In fact, as this chapter comes to a close, the first publicly available version of Whurlwind has been posted to Apple's official QuickDraw 3D site:

```
http://www.info.apple.com/qd3d/Viewer.HTML
```

This version now allows you to follow WWWAnchor nodes. The interface for this is characteristically simple: With any tool selected, when the cursor passes over a node grouped with a WWWAnchor node, the cursor changes to a finger pointing at a tiny radio button. Click on the button and Whurlwind sends a "GetURL" AppleEvent to Netscape.

As the weeks go by, we expect the appearance of other features in Whurlwind. We had an opportunity to speak to Bill Enright, one of its primary developers, and he had many exciting tidbits of information about where this viewer is going.

Bill's previous coding experience is a veritable "coat of many colors," with experience on network protocol stacks and custom vertical applications for a variety of companies. He says he took on Whurlwind to prove to himself that he is still a hacker, and from what we've seen we're compelled to agree.

Whurlwind's final interface will be augmented with a "fly tool," at the bottom of the viewer window. This will allow true 3-D scene navigation. The default QuickDraw 3D viewer is designed for viewing models, and won't let you approach them too closely, as is proper for a single object. For an entire scene, selecting the fly tool lets you zoom right into, over, and around the scene at will.

The model viewing mode will be retained, according to Bill, and perhaps autoselected, according to the context of the scene being viewed. This will let you navigate without requiring explicit control over the shifts in perspective involved (e.g., "inside" versus "outside").

Multiple light sources will also be added in the near future. Currently, Whurlwind applies a single light source to a scene for shading and supplies ambient light for overall illumination. The development plan calls for full support of multiple light sources, to support the greater flexibility provided by the 1.0 VRML specification.

For the average Internet VRML user, one of the most exciting new features planned is the ability for a scene to embed objects that are defined as WWWInline nodes. This lets parts of a large scene be loaded over the Net as needed, lessening VRML's obvious potential to choke a standard 14.4 or 28.8Kbps modem link. Whurlwind will soon integrate this feature, which may be the key to its widespread adoption outside the technical circles that have the higher-bandwidth connections necessary to make it scream today.

Another cool thing that the Whurlwind team has in the works is various modes for scene translations. Once you've opened a VRML scene in Whurlwind, it's currently possible to save it as a standard QuickDraw 3D 3DMF file. In the future, there may be a separate utility that would allow this translation to be a simple drag and drop operation.

As for translation in the other direction—from QuickDraw 3D file to VRML—the future is somewhat less clear. QvLib allows for only one-way translation, with no capability to turn a collection of its internal graphic objects back into a VRML scene graph. There are several efforts underway in the Mac and Internet developers communities to facilitate 3DMF translation to VRML, but no products have been announced yet.

Speaking with Bill, it was apparent that he is earnest in his desire to provide low-cost tools for Macintosh VRML development. Should these types of translation tools not materialize soon, we wouldn't be surprised to hear that he has something in the works in this area.

Finally, we heard that Whurlwind will add textures to its feature set soon, and his ideas about implementation methods are revolutionary. This may sound like hyperbole, but the architecture of the MacOS and its component parts may allow the team to do things with textures and moving images that simply aren't possible on other platforms.

The best news of all is that the timeline for all these additions and enhancements is such that, by the time you read this, they may already have become realities. The development team is on the crest of that wave of giddy, enthusiastic, creative energy that comes from developing code for a project that is both challenging and fun. Riding this wave allows programmers to bring us the coolest tools as quickly as possible.

Summary

As you can tell, we were excited by Whurlwind. As the lone VRML viewer for the Macintosh platform (as of this writing), this puts a lot of weight on the shoulders of its development team. Happily, those shoulders seem able to stand up to the challenge! Whurlwind's ease of use and tight integration with the MacOS, make this client simple, powerful, and useful.

One final plug: if you have a Mac, it behooves you to get this viewer—one look and you'll be hooked.

On a broader scale, our examination of VRML viewers has given us a good sense of VRML from the user's perspective. As a language, VRML definitely represents a revolution in the way we'll navigate and play on the Internet in the future. As a first attempt, it represents an impressive effort to use current bandwidth and computing resources to deliver rendered realities across the globe.

Nevertheless, we're compelled to point out how far from "state of the art" VRML really is. Let's look at the Virtual SOMA scene one more time, to see how this file originated in AutoCAD and 3DStudio (see Figure 5-6).

Figure 5-6: Virtual SOMA as originally designed in AutoCAD and 3DStudio.

There's no need to dissect VRML's shortcomings—they're readily apparent when you compare Figures 5-5 and 5-6. We don't intend to belittle VRML, or its creators' achievement in any way. We merely wish to temper your enthusiasm with a gentle reminder of how much further Virtual Reality has to go before it can truly live up to its name!

## CHAPTER 6

The VRML Windows
Browsers

In Their Infancy

he best VRML browsers available today are for UNIX platforms, particularly SGI machines, which can render images on-the-fly at an acceptable speed. Even though VRML was designed to be platform independent, the system that runs the viewer must be able to handle the mathematics and video processing involved to render a textured, realistic, three-dimensional image.

In the real-world most computer users don't have SGI Indy machines with T-1 connections. In fact, most people use Microsoft Windows and a 14.4 or perhaps a 28.8Kbps modem.

The vanguard VRML browser producers realize that because Windows is the most prevalent computer platform, its users represent the largest software market in the world.

The Micro-Majority

Since Microsoft Windows comes pre-installed on most of the PCs sold in America, it's easy to see how it could become the most widespread computer platform in the world. Netsurfer Communications, which publishes an ad-supported electronic newsletter about the Net called *The Netsurfer's Digest*, sends a questionnaire to each of its new subscribers. So far, they've received over 10,000 responses and according to their

Continued

survey, about 65% of all Internet users own a PC running MS Windows! This isn't necessarily their only platform, nor even their preferred platform, but it is an eye-opening look at just how many Windows users there really are. You can check out the survey for yourself at:

```
http://www.netsurf.com/surveys.html
```

This chapter explores three VRML browsers for Microsoft Windows systems: VRWeb for Windows, made by a consortium composed of IICM, NCSA, and the Gopher team of the University of Minnesota; WebSpace, the product of an alliance between SGI and Template Graphics Software; and WorldView for Windows, designed and developed by InterVista Software.

All of these browsers were in either alpha or beta releases when we tested them. If they were in alpha, they were pretty much raw code, with neither testing nor frills to offer. If they were in beta, then the authors of this book functioned as guinea pigs for their project testing. Commercial versions of these browsers should being to appear by the time this book arrives in bookstores in Fall, 1995.

All three of these browsers were tested and reviewed using the following PC configuration:

- 90MHz Pentium processor
- 32MB RAM
- 540MB hard drive
- SVGA 256-color video display, video card, and drivers
- Microsoft Windows NT 3.5 Advanced Server
- 3Com Etherlink III card connected to a thin-net backbone
- 28.8Kbps connection to the Internet routed through a FreeBSD UNIX system

VRWeb for Windows

Most people would be surprised if at least one of the development teams for VRWeb for Windows didn't get involved in producing a VRML browser. This triumvirate promises to deliver something great, and gives VRML more clout as an emerging Internet technology. The three players involved include the Institute for Information Processing and Computer-Supported New Media (IICM), the National Center for Supercomputing Applications (NCSA), and the Gopher development team from the University of Minnesota.

The Greatness of Graz

IICM, part of the Graz University of Technology in Austria, is responsible for the development of Hyper-G, an integrated Internet information retrieval platform. Hyper-G combines HTML, Gopher, and Hyper-G protocol services into a single package. It supports a mixture of multimedia data, including digital audio and video, as well as PostScript and 3-D scenes, all delivered from a single browser. You can find out more about Hyper-G and VRWeb at:

```
http://www.iicm.tu-graz.ac.at/
```

Super Computing Tools from NCSA

NCSA at the University of Illinois at Urbana-Champaign is a research center dedicated to advancing the technologies involved in high-performance computing, communications, and information for both educational institutions and corporations. NCSA is best known as the birthplace of Mosaic, the first graphics browser and NCSA *httpd,* the widely used Web server.

Go Golden Gophers!

The Gopher team from the University of Minnesota created the widely-used iconic Internet data retrieval system known as Gopher (it's named after their school mascot, in fact). With the release of GopherVR for UNIX and Macintosh, they've developed a Gopher browser that adds a 3-D front-end to existing Gopher servers (see Figure 6-1). GopherVR accesses data in the form of 3-D scenes that can really put the relationships between documents into perspective. If you're interested in learning more about GopherVR, it can be accessed at:

```
gopher://boombox.micro.umn.edu
```

Because VRWeb is being developed by three nonprofit government-sponsored entities it (like NCSA *Mosaic)* is free to the public for end-users. The copyrighted source code will also be made available to

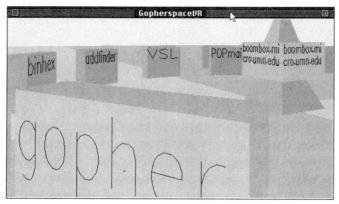

Figure 6-1: A look at the University of Minnesota's Gopher site through 3-D gopher-space with TurboGopherVR for the Mac.

non-commercial users at no charge. VRWeb is being touted as a platform for further research and experimentation into virtual reality systems, and as a means for educational institutions to visualize data in 3-D form.

VRWeb: The Early Days...

As we were writing this book, no commercial version of VRWeb was available. However, the lead developer for VRWeb for Windows was kind enough to provide an early release for us to review. It's available via anonymous ftp at:

```
ftp://fiicm1pc46.tu-graz.ac.at/ftp/vrshots
```

By the time you read this, VRWeb for Windows should be officially released, and may no longer be available at this location. In that case, please refer back to the Web site for Hyper-G to find the latest VRWeb information:

```
http://www.iicm.tu-graz.ac.at/
```

What You Need: More Is Better

Because VRWeb for Windows hasn't been released yet, there are still no instructions available for its use, nor a list of required software or hardware. Although it's hard to judge performance from such an early version, it's probably a good idea to help the software along with as powerful a PC as you can afford to throw at it (there's a lot going on under the hood of a VRML rendering program).

You'll probably need at least a 66MHz 80486 processor, a minimum of 12MB RAM, and definitely a 256-color SVGA display, video card, and driver. There are separate versions of VRWeb for Windows NT and Windows 3.1 (including Windows 3.11 and Windows 95).

If you're using Windows 3.1, you'll need to install Win32s. Win32s is a Microsoft subsystem that lets 32-bit programs—like VRWeb—run in a 16-bit environment (such as Windows 3.1 or 3.11). Windows for Workgroups 3.11 includes the Win32s subsystem, and Windows 95 is already a 32-bit operating system so it doesn't need Win32s.

If you need this software, you can download Win32s from:

```
ftp://ftp.outer.net/pub/mswindows/win32s.zip
```

You may also want to use Netscape or NCSA Mosaic to integrate with VRWeb so that it will launch seamlessly and load the requested file when you click on a hyperlink to a site with a ".WRL" file. To do this, you must set up a new MIME type in your Web browser. Here is an example for setting up Netscape to launch VRWeb for Windows:

1. Choose Preferences from the Options menu.
2. Choose Helper Applications from the pulldown menu.
3. Click the New Type button.
4. Go to the Configure New MIME Type dialog box:
   a. MIME Type should be: "x-world"
   b. MIME Subtype should be: "x-vrml"
5. For the Extensions field, you should enter: ".WRL".
6. In the Action selection box, click Launch Application.
7. For the application, select: "pathToVRWeb\vrw_win.exe".

What is MIME?

Multipurpose Internet Mail Extensions (MIME) is a convenient way to send and receive multimedia data over the Internet. MIME *content-types* are essentially a protocol header, sent in plain text format, that announce to an application what type of data is about to be sent. If the application knows how to handle the content-type, then it will—for example, a Web browser like Mosaic will know how to handle the *text/html* content-type. If the application runs into a type it can't handle, then it may call upon a helper application to take over and use the data. Windows users will often have to

Continued
configure helper applications in their Web browsers in order to play MPEG movies or WAV sound files delivered from the WWW.

Getting Around: Thumbs Up on the Heads Up

The VRWeb browser itself is based on the Harmony scene viewer which is part of Hyper-G (see Figure 6-2). Its face looks like that of any other Windows application: just the typical Windows border with menu selections up top, and relatively few other controls. In fact, just by looking at it, you would have no idea what it does.

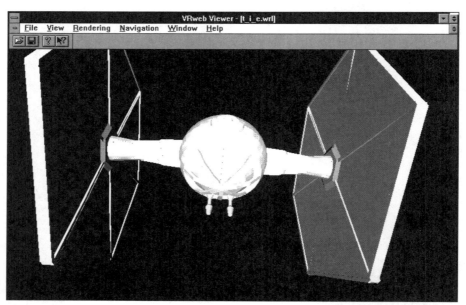

Figure 6-2: A look at VRWeb's interface, showing a rendered model of a TIE Fighter.

Most of the controls in VRWeb are concentrated in the pulldown menu items, rather than in buttons, control panels, or the like. The File menu item, obviously, lets you open a VRML ".WRL" file on your computer, or open a URL path to a ".WRL" file. It will also let you save the VRML source of any 3-D world you are viewing. View toggles the button menu bar on and off, and controls whether you want a hyperlink name to display when your mouse pointer is over a "hot" model.

The Rendering menu item lets you select in what detail you would like to view the objects. The simplest level of rendering is wireframe, which speeds up the drawing time considerably, but doesn't give the subtleties of texture and shading. The next level is rendering with faces, which gives you the added information of texture and color, but doesn't smooth the object, so a globe would look faceted like a cut stone, rather than a sphere.

Rendering an object as smooth gives you the most detail, and thus the most realism. Which level you choose depends on how much information you need about the world or 3-D model you are viewing. If you are navigating about in a virtual environment, such as the GopherSpace in GopherVR, then a wireframe or object-with-faces level of detail would more than likely be fine for you, and speed up the time it takes to draw the information. On the other hand, if you are a geological researcher in need of more information about rock formations around Mt. St. Helens, you will probably want smoothing, and thus the richest detail on the mountainsides you are viewing.

The Navigation menu lets you select how you want to interact with the virtual world. Fly mode lets you move about the world in practically any direction, by holding down the left mouse button and dragging it over the display window. Fly mode is ideal if you want to move up or down, to get a view of the world from a different angle. In Walk mode, you are allowed to move around the world as if you were walking: You can go forwards, backwards, left, or right, but not up or down.

The final Navigation selection is Heads Up, a group of four icons that appear in the center of the display window and allow you to quickly and easily select the action you want to perform (see Figure 6-3). The top icon looks like two eyes and lets you fly around a scene. To walk, select a picture of a person walking.

The third icon, which looks like compass arrows, moves the camera along the x- and y-axis. The bottommost icon, which looks like a crosshair, allows you to target a 3-D model and quickly zoom towards it The fact that the Heads Up display focuses all of the movement features into a single strip of icons overlaying the image makes this browser simple to use.

Figure 6-3: VRWeb's Heads Up controls.

Performance: Is VRWeb the Tortoise in this Race?

We don't want to treat VRWeb for Windows too roughly on its performance. Given that optimization is one of the last polishing tasks before making a package commercial, it's probably fair to say that the overall performance of VRWeb is good. What it lacks in sheer rendering speed (and the pre-release version lacks a bit) it makes up for in its simple and intuitive user interface.

But in some ways, VRWeb's quick-and-easy interface could be a detriment: you often find yourself whizzing around a 3-D model much faster than VRWeb can recalculate its position and re-render the image.

It seems that the initial version of VRWeb for Windows is probably best-suited for navigation around a simple worldspace, or the manipulation of the simplest (perhaps 20-50 polygons) 3-D models. There is, however, a skillful and talented group of developers working on this browser's various platforms. So, despite its current speed deficiencies and Spartan appearance, judging by past accomplishments we expect great things from VRWeb in the future.

WebSpace for Windows

Of course you'd expect SGI, whose Open Inventor rendering language is the lifeblood of VRML, to have a presence in the VRML browser scene. WebSpace is part of their WebFORCE WWW author/server solution, which includes SGI hardware and software. The SGI WebSpace home page can be found at:

```
http://www.sgi.com/Products/WebFORCE/WebSpace/
```

Silicon Graphics itself is only producing WebSpace for SGI platforms. It has left the development for all other platforms to Template Graphics Software. Information about WebSpace for Windows and other platforms can be retrieved from Template Graphics' WebSpace page at:

```
http://www.sd.tgs.com/~template/WebSpace/monday.html
```

We reviewed WebSpace v1.0b1 (beta 1), currently available only for Windows NT. However, Windows 3.1 and Windows 95 versions are already well underway (but neither one has been assigned a prospective beta release date at this time). You can download the Windows NT version directly from:

```
ftp://ftp.sd.tgs.com/pub/template/WebSpace/WinNT/WS32N10B.EXE
```

No support is available for the beta version unless you register with Template Graphics for $49.00. Registration includes a free upgrade to the final version of WebSpace V1.0 when it's released. Keep tabs on this site for information about the other Windows versions, too—it's just a matter of time before they're ready!

What You Need: Forget It, Get the Pentium

Until the Windows 3.1 and Windows 95 versions are released, you'll need to run WebSpace for Windows on NT 3.5 or higher. In addition, because WebSpace is a Microsoft Visual C++ application, you'll need the standard DLLs for the Visual C++ runtime libraries, MFC, and OLE. If you already have Microsoft Visual C++ 2.1 installed on your NT system, then you don't have to worry about it. Otherwise, you'll need to download them from Template Graphics:

```
ftp://ftp.sd.tgs.com/pub/template/WebSpace/WinNT/WIN32-DLL.EXE
```

The minimum system requirements to run WebSpace for Windows are: a 66MHz 486 processor, 8 to 16MB RAM, and a 256-color SVGA display system. However, the preferred system is a 90Mhz Pentium (or faster) with 16MB RAM and a 24-bit high-resolution TrueColor graphics card. Based on our experiences in using this browser, the latter system with a standard local-bus or PCI SVGA graphics card, instead of the 24-bit card, is probably quite adequate.

Finally, you'll also want a Web browser (Netscape or Mosaic) that can launch WebSpace for Windows as a helper application. WebSpace for Windows cannot view URLs without the pass-through assistance of a

Web browser, though it can view local files. The instructions for setting up Netscape to launch WebSpace are the same as for VRWeb; simply replace the VRWeb path and filename with WebSpace's.

Getting Around: Full of Features

WebSpace for Windows has a unique interface compared to the other two browsers we examined. You use a visual representation of the "console deck" of a cybervehicle to pilot around the virtual world or 3-D model. There are two different types of views in which you use this vehicle: the Walk View and the Examiner View, (see Figures 6-4, 6-5, and 6-6) both of which are selectable under the View pulldown menu.

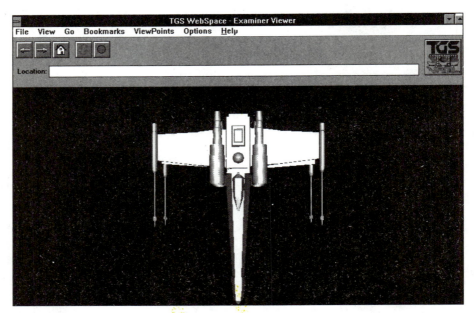

Figure 6-4: WebSpace displaying a rendered X-Wing fighter.

The Walk View gives you the ability to move around in the virtual world as if you were walking through it (or driving through it in your cybervehicle). It doesn't allow you to "fly" around a scene, but lets you move left, right, forward, and backward on a level horizontal plane.

Movement is controlled by clicking and dragging your mouse pointer on the representation of a T-shaped Joystick in the middle of your virtual console deck. On the right side of the Joystick handle is a Tilt Knob that tilts the camera up, down, right, or left. You can use this feature to scan a scene without moving, just like moving your head around.

To the immediate right of the Joystick itself is an Arrow Pad, that moves the camera along the x- and y-axis of your orientation. The Arrow Pad doesn't change the tilt of the camera, only its position in space. To the Joystick's left is a Seek Tool that can be used to quickly zoom towards a particular object. Activating the Seek Tool by clicking on it causes the cursor to change into a target that is used to select the object you want to move toward.

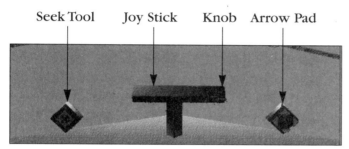

Figure 6-5: The console deck for WebSpace's Walk View.

The Examiner View allows you to manipulate a 3-D model, rather than move around a world. Movement of the object is achieved via the use of a virtual Trackball on the console deck. In using the Trackball it's best to imagine that the object or scene you are manipulating is actually inside the Trackball, as if it were encased in a solid glass globe.

Any movement of the Trackball is equivalent to a movement of the object in the viewer window. To the right of the Trackball is a Thumbwheel that acts as a virtual dolly control and moves the camera in or out of the viewspace. The Examiner View also has an Arrow Pad and a Seek Tool, which behave in the same manner as the ones in the Walk View.

Every movement option in both the Walk and Examiner Views has a corresponding shortcut keystroke, a keystroke-plus-mouse movement, or a button-click equivalent.

Other nice features included in WebSpace for Windows are a VRML history (kept separate from the histories in other Web browsers), user-defined vantage points for particular scenes, three levels of rendering detail (low/wireframe, no textures, and full), and three levels of speed for user movement.

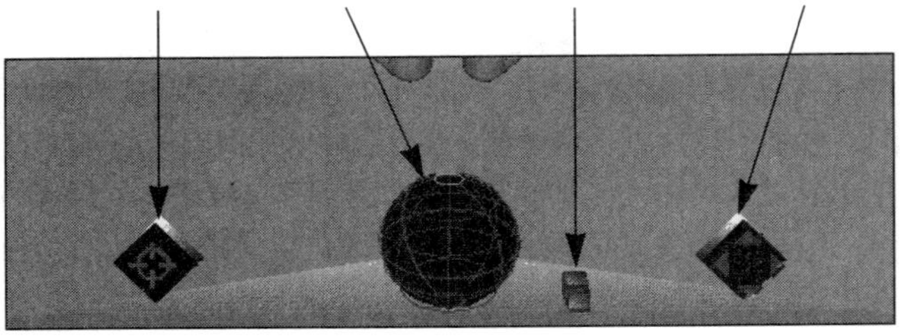

Seek Tool Track Ball   Thumbwheel Arrow Pad

Figure 6-6: The console deck for WebSpace's Examiner View.

Performance: Will It Get Better?

WebSpace for Windows has a multitude of beautiful features and a versatile and interesting user interface, but can be slow enough to be disconcerting, on occasion. You'll sometimes find yourself making a movement, waiting for several seconds, and then watching the rendered image refresh itself.

It's the same pattern of frustration that many Internet users experience when browsing a graphics-laden WWW site on the Internet with a 14.4Kbps modem. Nothing seems to move fast enough, you begin to get bored, and you finally decide, "What's the use?" and then bail out altogether.

The good news is that this isn't the final release. Template Graphics still has plenty of time to optimize their code and make it faster. In fact, they already claim that the final 1.0 release will be significantly improved over the pre-release we examined. Template Graphics also plans on supporting other rendering engines in the future, including Microsoft's RealityLab rendering software, which is the same as that used in the next—and fastest—VRML Windows browser.

WorldView for Windows

WorldView for Windows is the first effort of InterVista Software, a company led by Tony Parisi who, along with Mark Pesci, was a principle architect of the VRML 1.0 standard. Most VRML browsers are written for rendering engines, for a good reason: the raw number-crunching power needed for rendering VRML models is readily available on this type of platform. InterVista's primary goal is to be first-to-market with a fast and viable VRML browser for Microsoft Windows, to claim the lion's share of this largest of all computer markets.

To accomplish its goal of providing a high-speed rendering solution for Windows, InterVista has integrated the technology of Microsoft's RealityLab rendering engine into its product, as well as making it network-aware. According to InterVista, with WorldView, a standard PC, and a 14.4 modem, users can interact with a virtual environment in real-time.

For this book, we reviewed the 0.8 Alpha 1 version of WorldView for Windows, for which no end-user support is currently offered. It is available at the following URL:

```
http://www.webmaster.com/vrml
```

The fully supported version is due for release in late August, 1995 and will be distributed by Infinite Light, Inc. for $49.95. Infinite Light's home page is at:

```
http://www.vrml.com/index.html
```

What You Need: A VRML Browser for the Rest of Us

WorldView for Windows operates with every one of the Windows platforms, which many of the others do not—at least not yet. The principle platform is Microsoft Windows NT 3.5 and 3.51, but it also works well with the other Windows platforms, and runs under Windows 3.1, Windows for Workgroups 3.11, or Windows 95.

The Alpha version of WorldView has the distinction of requiring only relatively modest hardware for a VRML browser. The minimum suggested processor is a 50MHz 80486. InterVista recommends 8MB RAM, though you'll probably want at least 12 MB for a Windows 3.1 or 3.11 system, especially when running WorldView as a helper application to a memory-hungry Web browser such as Netscape.

If you're running Windows NT or Windows 95, then you'll probably want a minimum of 16 MB. As usual, you'll also want a 256-color display driver and video graphics card to appreciate the nuances of the textures and shading of WorldView's rendered images. As with VRWeb, if you're running Windows 3.1, you'll need to install Win32s.

Once again, you might want to use Netscape or Mosaic to interface to WorldView, because many ".WRL" files will be launched from HTML documents. The section on VRWeb explains how to configure Netscape for the VRML MIME type. If you are only going to visit VRML sites, however, you don't need another WWW browser, because WorldView is WinSock compliant, and doesn't require a WWW browser to handle its URLs.

Getting Around: It's Just a Click Away

Like VRWeb and WebSpace, WorldView also has a pulldown menu bar with an assortment of nice features (See Figure 6-7). You can select rendering detail, save ".WRL" files, place bookmarks on visited sites, and control several other options that affect performance and setup. In most of these areas WorldView doesn't set itself apart from the other three VRML browsers.

The best thing about WorldView is its slick operation via a control panel at the bottom of the application window. There are controls to *move, tilt, translate,* and *fly,* as well as switch between a Walk View and a Model View. Essentially, you use the Model View when you want to manipulate a 3-D model, and the Walk View when you want to move within the 3-D worldspace around the model.

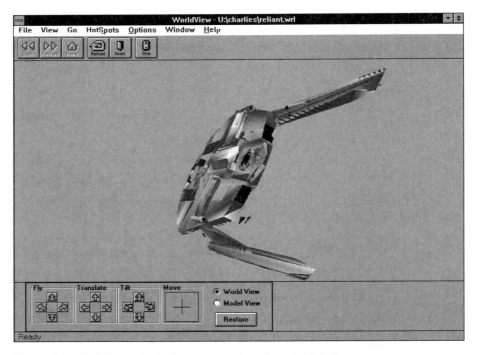

Figure 6-7: WorldView displaying a rendering of the USS Reliant.

Movement operates the same for both the Walk and Model Views, but in the Walk View you're the one who's flying around, while in the Model View it's the 3-D object that's doing the flying. The movement control panel is a pad with a crosshair in the middle of it. You track the mouse pointer along while holding down the left mouse button. Moving the pointer above the crosshair moves you forward; moving it behind the crosshair moves you backward. Moving it to the right of the crosshair rotates to the right, moving it to the left rotates to the left. You can also pan by holding down the Shift key while moving the mouse, or change your pitch by holding down the Control key while moving the mouse.

Flying, translating, and tilting are controlled using arrow buttons on the control panel. These three operations behave differently in the Walk and Model Views, but support easy, intuitive navigation around VRML scenes. This software is definitely worth a try!

Performance: Breaking Records

After its control panel, the next best thing about WorldView is its overall speed: it is probably the fastest of the Windows VRML browsers that we reviewed. Is it because of the Microsoft RealityLab integration? Because it uses faster rendering algorithms? Or because it was designed by Parisi, who helped develop the VRML 1.0 specification?

It's probably a combination of all of these: high-quality code plus dedication, and a true understanding of the program's intended behavior. The ".WRL" file loading time is probably WorldView's greatest bottleneck. Once an image is loaded, you'll have no problem moving around the world or manipulating an object. You'll experience some lag time when loading larger and more colorful models, but compared to other browsers it moves quite quickly. At this rate, InterVista will probably cash in on the Windows market share they so obviously covet.

By the way, don't let WorldView's smoke-and-mirrors of the spinning earth fool you—it may behave like a VRML model, but it really isn't! But since it was developed by one of the VRML co-authors, who knows; maybe it will be in the VRML 2.0 spec.

A Look Back

We've explored three VRML browsers that are nearing release for the Microsoft Windows platform: VRWeb for Windows, WebSpace for Windows, and WorldView for Windows. You've learned that they are all still in alpha or beta, but that most of them will be commercial releases by Fall, 1995.

Remember, these browsers handle only VRML. For other Web services, you'll still need a WWW browser like NCSA Mosaic or Netscape, and you've learned how to configure the latter to incorporate the VRML MIME type. Most of these VRML browsers offer essentially the same functionality but with different techniques and representations. We've explored this functionality further and learned how to navigate through a virtual scene with each one, or how to manipulate a 3-D model.

Finally, we've looked at how each VRML browser performs as a rendering engine and 3-D world viewer. Although this chapter wasn't written as a competition among these browsers, you may be asking which one is the best.

VRWeb for Windows, WebSpace for Windows, and WorldView for Windows all stand on their own very well. But when it comes to speed on the Windows platform, InterVista Software's WorldView clearly leads the others. By designing their first release of the browser for Windows, instead of porting code from an X Windows or SGI platform, they've incorporated the best technologies available for that platform to create a browser that almost creates the illusion of virtual reality.

Because all of these browsers are still in alpha or beta, we hasten to add that these speed differences could disappear or even shift completely. But, if you're using Windows and had to make a choice today, we'd recommend WorldView.

All of these browsers are more focused and cohesive than most emerging standards. They all offer interesting and unique user interfaces; they are all developed by solid teams who are acknowledged leaders in the field of high-end graphics or Internet information representation systems; and they are all at the forefront of a new Internet technology. If these represent the first steps along this new road, then we are in for an exciting trip!

Where Will They Go from Here?

The next obvious avenue for VRML browsers would be to integrate OLE and DDE into their interfaces. Imagine being able to pull a VRML world directly off your browser and drag it directly onto your favorite raytracing program so that you could manipulate it!

Perhaps another development would be the direct integration of VRML into the Microsoft Windows Network environment. In this scenario, you'd be able to pull up a user's system from your network simply by clicking on it. When you did this, a VRML representation of that system would be created, showing shared folders as open filing cabinets, and unshared ones as locked. When you looked into a shared filing cabinet, you'd see each of its filing folders, which would represent the individual files or directories underneath. Pull one out, and a copy of the data would instantly be transferred to your machine!

Currently this is all academic, since most of the VRML browsers haven't yet been released, and the VRML specification remains at version 1.0. There are infinitely many possibilities that are yet to be explored, including many that are not specific to the Windows environment. These will probably include the integration of object motion, user-to-object interactions, object-to-object interactions, and user-to-user interactions, along with simulcast sound to accompany such scenes. But before they can advance into these areas, VRML trailblazers need to gain a firm footing. That's where the next section comes into play!

Section

Three

VRML Vistas

he third section includes Chapters 7 through 10, with visits to three state-of-the-art VRML sites in Chapters 7 through 9, concluding with a speculative rumination on the present and future capabilities of VRML (or other similar 3-D representational languages that may succeed it).

This part of the book begins in Chapter 7, "Post Modern VRML," with a visit to a stunning experiment in hypermedia known as WAXweb. It then moves on in Chapter 8, "The Virtual Vegas Online VRML Site," to visit what can only be described as an entertainment-oriented gambling and arcade atmosphere right there on the Internet! Your site visits conclude with Chapter 9, "Virtually There...," a stop at an architecturally-oriented virtual world, situated in the real world in the Variety Arts Center, in Los Angeles.

Each visit offers more than a guided tour of the site's capabilities and attractions. We also discuss the design techniques and approaches employed to build these sites. Each visit recounts the major problems the designers encountered, their primary implementation issues, and describes any special-purpose tools they built or used as workarounds.

After a look at these VRML implementations, we turn speculative in Chapter 10, "The Future of VRML." Here, we explore VRML's potential, and try to recommend appropriate applications based on its current capabilities. After a broad discussion of VRML's shortcomings, we discuss ongoing and planned research and implementation directions, both for VRML itself and for related languages, development environments, and tools. Throughout, we refer to concrete examples, and point to readily-accessible Web sites wherever possible. Finally, we supply a compendium of useful VRML-related Web resources to help you find the latest and greatest information about VRML in particular, and virtual reality in general.

## CHAPTER 7

Post-Modern VRML
WAX on the WWW

*i*n our exploration of VRML and its current incarnations on the Internet, you've seen a great deal of imagination and innovation displayed by the early adopters of this technology. The most unique implementation we've encountered lives at the WWW site known as *WAXweb*.

A highly complex Web site in every respect, WAXweb inherits its artistic depth from previous iterations of the project called "WAX or the discovery of television among the bees" or, more simply, "WAX." This project is an experimental piece of what artist David Blair calls hypermedia—content that is delivered on a number of different media in parallel or sequentially.

With WAXweb, David Blair and his cohorts have developed a custom application that delivers the latest, most thoroughly collaborative, networked incarnation of the WAX project. This particular evolutionary stage of the project includes HTML-formatted text, a MOO, video, images, and VRML objects and scenes. All these elements interact intimately, where each one blends into the others, and all are combined, shuffled, and recombined on-the-fly. Out of this intermingling arises a truly singular narrative, the story of WAX.

It's important to explore the history of the project and its creators to gain a better understanding of the specific design requirements faced by the WAXweb team, and how they adapted the Web and VRML to their unique requirements. (One stylistic note: for clarity, we'll use "WAX" to refer to the project as a whole in its many forms, and "WAXweb" as the specific incarnation of WAX on the WWW, with VRML components.)

Once your foundation for understanding WAX is established, we'll look at the WAXweb site. Our investigation will range from the translation of scenes into VRML, to the separation and organization of individual scenes into their component objects, to the custom HTTP server that handles user requests, and finally to the MOO that acts as the glue that holds it all together.

We'll close with an attempt to place WAXweb in the context of VRML, as it exists on the Internet today, and into the future. David Blair is working to realize ambitious goals with WAXweb, above and beyond the scope of the creation as a work of art. We'll attempt to do this grand vision justice in the context of our own project, the VRML book you hold in your hands!

Born in the Stacks

David Blair traces the history of WAX back to his days spent as a librarian for the state of New York. Here he explored video works available through the public library system, and discovered a number of pieces that started him thinking about video as an artistic medium.

What Blair found was an ideal voice for the type of art he wanted to create, the type of works he had been trying to express through traditional narrative films. His earliest attempts were self-described "grotesques," that "...often winked at the viewer while describing the processes of their own creation" (Blair, WAXweb Mosaic-MOO article, 1994).

This type of fictional narrative fits squarely into the post-modern style, a style often characterized by an attempt to escape linear, expository narrative by breaking down standard structures and methods used in traditional art to create the illusion of "reality." The particular form that most interested Blair is specifically known to as "meta-fiction."

It is into this defining slot that WAX most comfortably fits. Both its narrative and images are considered "processed" by the author, in the sense that neither attempts to allow their raw materials to exist in their natural state within the work. The images that Blair created are entirely electronic—most of the 2000 individual shots traversed a series of digital post-processes or were actually created by analog and digital synthesis.

The text for WAX was likewise coerced via post-processing. His raw materials originated from directed random readings and accidental connections between elements. These were then combined and shaped on a personal computer, using standard cut-and-paste techniques.

Both text and images were developed simultaneously over a period of six years, and then brought together using a Montage non-linear editing system. At this point, the content of WAX existed as video, which was then distributed in the form of 16mm film. It thereby earned the distinction of being the first independent feature film to be constructed on the Montage system. It is in this incarnation that Blair's work is properly referred to as "WAX or the discovery of television among the bees" (85 minutes in length, 1991).

It was Blair's intention from early stages to create WAX as a hybrid work of art, translating and transporting it to as many different media as seemed appropriate. The stage that immediately followed its release as a film was an experiment in collaborative hypertext authoring using an application called "StorySpace." This application was developed by Jay Bolter, author of the book *Writing Space: The Computer, Hypertext and the History of Writing*, among others.

Bolter's idea of narrative as a form of travel through a spatial realization of a fictional topography appealed to Blair. By porting WAX into StorySpace, Blair could escape from the linearity demanded by the medium of film. This inspired Blair to create WAX's narrative as a hyperlinked space that readers could explore.

The translation process required the creation of 600 nodes to correspond to the number of dialog lines in the film. Since almost all of this dialog is in narrative form, it lends itself well to a hypertext medium. These nodes were fleshed out with descriptions of the 2000 or so shots that comprised the film, with the shots of a particular passage linked to its corresponding text component.

Blair then selected 25 writers worldwide to collaborate on the project. Together, they all worked on expanding the totality of the narrative. StorySpace possesses a certain degree of groupware functionality, but when the authors needed to increase their level of interaction, they turned to the Internet.

Genesis of WAXweb

WAX in StorySpace

The Internet offered its entire suite of familiar tools to aid the group's collaboration: person-to-person e-mail, a private ftp site, and a mailing list. When synchronous conferencing was required, they used telnet to connect to a MOO or MUD (Multi-User Dungeon), an Internet-based role-playing game.

A MOO is a programmable, extensible version of a MUD, in effect a multi-user, text-based virtual reality. Blair was struck by the similarity between the MOO's maze of rooms and a web of hyperlinked text. Both are topologies that are navigated by the individual in a more-or-less random order. In the course of each such traversal, a unique narrative arises. It was this type of voyage that Blair wished for his readers, as they picked their way through the individual nodes, or rooms, that comprised WAX. For each visit, the unique series of choices and coincidences would result in an entirely new narrative for each explorer.

That the next step in WAXweb's evolution arose out of pure coincidence is appropriate, given that WAX's narratives also depend on random connections in time and space. The MOO used by the StorySpace authors, the Hypertext Hotel MOO, was administered by Tom Meyer, himself amidst development of intriguing extensions to the MOO system.

This MOO was in turn based on Steven White's MOO source code, but Meyer was actively modifying source code, and adding utilities, filters, and other tools to mold the application to his own designs. The first augmentation that ultimately caused Blair's and Meyer's paths to converge was a filter for importing StorySpace files into the MOO. This filter converted nodes into rooms and the links between nodes into passages between rooms. At the same time, Meyer adapted the command set of the MOO to more closely resemble that of a hypertext authoring application.

Blair decided that WAX should move from StorySpace to take up residence on the MOO. He and the other authors would lose the simple graphical interface that the application afforded, but would gain full-time synchronous collaboration on a global scale that could only be supported by the MOO.

WAX has since moved onto its own RS/6000 running its own MOO server. Even so, the original Hypertext Hotel MOO is still in operation, and its members still concern themselves with issues surrounding collaborative hypertext authoring. You can find the Hypertext Hotel MOO at:

```
telnet://duke.cs.brown.edu:8888/
```

WAX on the MOO

With its new residence on a MOO, WAX became accessible to anyone with a telnet client, and no longer dependent on a desktop machine's ability to run StorySpace. Additionally, its authoring and collaboration tools were integrated into a single virtual architecture. This effectively opened up the potential pool of collaborators to the entire populace of the Internet, a prospect welcomed by Blair. He expected the addition of masses of contributors to create a corresponding increase in the creative potential of the poetry machine called WAX.

Since its initial migration from film to hypertext, WAX had been stripped of any visual components. The images of the film had been distilled into the shot descriptions that linked to portions of dialog. Meyer's next modification to the Hypertext Hotel MOO let Blair reintegrate those images into the text.

Meyer realized that the only effective multimedia vehicle on the Internet was the World Wide Web. Further, he understood that the only way to preserve the MOO's authoring environment was to join the two into a hybrid of Internet services. To achieve this, Meyer started with some help from the people behind ChibaMOO, another MOO available through the Web at:

```
http://www.sensemedia.net/sprawl/11
```

WAX on the Web

From the ChibaMOO, Meyer acquired the source code out of which grew a customized HTTP server written in Perl. This code translates HTTP requests into a form recognizable by the MOO. This makes the MOO available through the Web while retaining its underlying architecture, without having to write an entire suite of CGI scripts to do translation or act as a gateway. Instead, the URLs that point to particular objects within the MOO are referenced with simple token/value pairs, as in:

```
http://bug.village.virginia.edu/obj=1776
```

This reference retrieves the default entry point to the site when a registered user logs in. The URL is parsed and passed to the MOO, which interprets the token/value pairs, and then retrieves the relevant objects, while performing any necessary translations. The data returned to the client constructs the page shown in Figure 7-1.

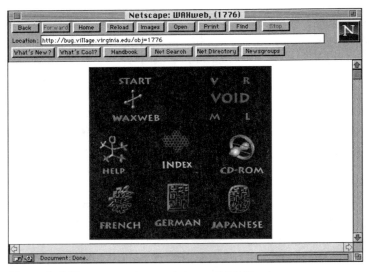

Figure 7-1: The user welcome screen at WAXweb.

The ability to reference any object in the MOO database with a simple query string lends tremendous power to WAXweb. The "obj=" portion of the URL refers to the method by which the viewer wishes to access the object. The default method is HTML, which extracts SGML-encoded text from the object and translates it to HTML on-the-fly, and inserts appropriate hypertext links to images, sounds, and other objects as it goes.

The extensibility of the interaction between the Web and the MOO emerges from the database, which lets any amount of information be attached to a given object in the MOO. It even allows additional methods to be added at will. For example, to add VRML to WAXweb, Meyer added VRML code to all relevant objects and simply created a new method, referenced in the URL as "vrml=" (with the corresponding object's number after the equal sign).

This implementation preserved the MOO's synchronous, interactive, hypertext authoring environment—making WAX available to the Web as a kind of virtual, dynamic HTML document, complete with sounds, pictures, and movie clips. With this development, WAX became WAXweb.

Meyer and Blair, with the help of Suzanne Hader and others at Brown University, turned the concepts of the Web, MOOs, and narrative inside out, and thoroughly intermingled them. In the process, they implemented some good design decisions. Along the way, the MOO became a kind of programmable, relational, multimedia database that held digital images and sounds in addition to SGML and VRML files. This functionality enhances its native ability to host multi-user interaction in a text-based virtual reality.

As we mentioned earlier, a custom HTTP server written in Perl serves as the go-between for Web browsers wanting to access the MOO. With total control over the way the MOO supports the HTTP protocol, WAXWeb opens the door to many potential capabilities; the WAXweb team has done a good job of capitalizing on them.

Since the site allows users to register and log in using a unique name for each visit, the MOO server can keep track of any user's specific state. All registered users are presented with an interface that allows for customization of the WAXweb's interface, as shown in Figure 7-2.

The ability to keep track of a viewer's preferences brings a new and previously unused capability to the Web. Given the wide variance among the platforms used to browse, this is definitely a desirable function. If you compound this variation with the heavy reliance on platform resources integral to VRML, the ability to customize a site to its users' capabilities becomes an absolute necessity.

Beyond allowing users to set certain viewing options, the MOO infrastructure underlying WAXweb brings an entirely new level of interaction to the Web. Users can add and delete bookmarks that point to specific WAX pages that reside on the WAXweb server. Comments can be added to a current page, and the other Wax users' comments are visible. In addition, users have the choice of opening a link interface, as shown in Figure 7-3.

This interface supports some of the collaborative hypertext authoring available from the MOO through WAX's presence on the Web. Users can

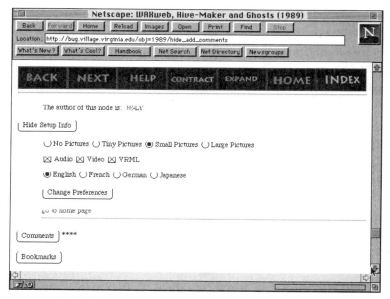

Figure 7-2: WAXweb's interface customization settings.

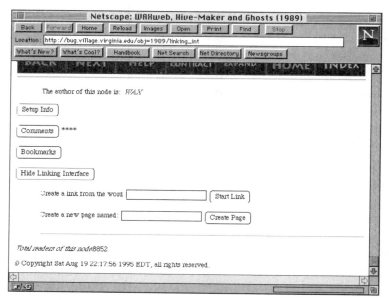

Figure 7-3: WAXweb's link interface.

add links from words on the current page to other pages in WAXweb, and even create entirely new pages. By allowing users to create new

Web pages at will, WAXweb's keepers have supplied the Internet public with another home for their WWW authoring attempts.

Finally, the WAXweb architects constructed several intelligent mirrors of WAXweb's multimedia portions. Binary resources embedded in the HTML versions of MOO rooms are duplicated on a number of geographically dispersed Web servers. When a user connects to WAXweb's main server at:

```
http://bug.village.virginia.edu/
```

his or her point of origin is examined and the closest mirror site determined. From then on, any HTML that's generated on-the-fly has all its HREF pointers directed to the mirror site. In this way, all the HTML is generated at a single site and the resources the code points to can be retrieved from elsewhere. This extends the main WAXweb server's ability to serve the masses, without getting bogged down with requests for images or sounds.

Now that we've discussed the historical, creative, and technical underpinnings of WAXweb, let's look at the VRML portions of WAX. Since its very beginning, WAX has included numerous 3-D scenes as part of its narrative. It is only recently, however, that these scenes have been reintegrated with the form WAX has taken on the Internet.

WAX in VRML

The scenes Blair used in the original film version of WAX were created in 1990 over a period of nine months by Florence Ormezzano on an Amiga. When asked about translation problems, Blair said they paled in comparison to the difficulties involved with creating the worlds at that early stage of modeling/rendering technology. He has been pleased with the advances made since then and development of the worlds for his next film, *Jews in Space*, is proceeding much more quickly than those early experiments.

In brief, in early spring of 1995, the original files were transported through a number of machines and translated from the original Amiga files to DXF and then to Inventor format. From there, Meyer and Hader wrote a MOO-scripted utility to parse Inventor files and break them up into individual nodes. The criteria for a node is defined as including a single IndexedFaceSet and its associated points. Breaking up a scene into its components allows for extra flexibility in the way WAXweb uses VRML.

A single node is a simple object node, like the one pictured in
Figure 7-4.

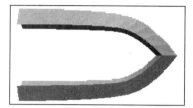

Figure 7-4: A single whale bone from the Archtune VRML scene.

The benefits of this method are twofold. First, an entire VRML scene,
when delivered to its user, can actually be constructed on-the-fly. The
component ".wrl" files reside on a separate HTTP server (here again,
this extends WAXweb's ability to serve as many concurrent users as
possible). An entire scene can be constructed from WWWInline nodes
and relative transform nodes. Second, a scene's transforms may be modified and its embedded WWWAnchor node values changed by interpreted MOO code on demand.

We're going to show you a portion of the VRML source from an
introductory VRML scene, entitled "Archtune." Its URL is:

```
http://bug.village.virginia.edu/obj=3742
```

In the code you'll see references to the eight ribs of a whale on a
separate server, with transforms between each rib. You can see how the
entire scene looks in Figure 7-5.

Here's the code:

```
#VRML V1.0 ascii

DEF Viewer Info { string "examiner" }
DEF Title Info { string "WAXweb, THIS IS ARCHTUNE (3742)" }
DEF BackgroundColor Info { string "0 0 0" }

Separator {
  Switch { whichChild 0
    DEF View_1
      PerspectiveCamera {
        position 5596.54 -85847.9 -444723
        orientation 0.209572 0.456594 -0.864639  1.62061
        focalDistance 219683}
```

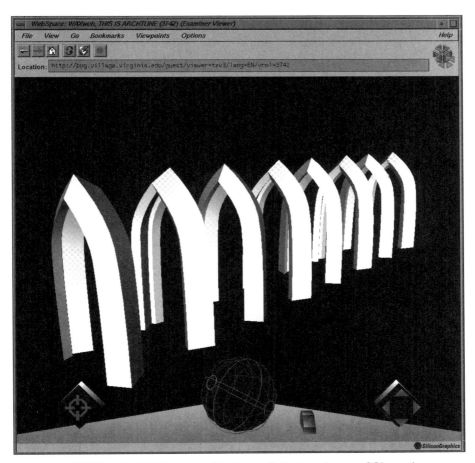

Figure 7-5: WAXweb's VRML scene, "Archtune," displayed on an SGI running Netscape 1.1 and WebSpace.

```
# the preceding sets up the viewpoint and info fields for the
# entire scene. Now we'll begin loading the eight ribs in
# WWWInline nodes.
  }
 Separator {
  Separator {
   WWWAnchor {
    name "http://bug.village.virginia.edu/vrml=3743"
    WWWInline {
```

```
        name
"http://jefferson.village.virginia.edu/wax/media/vrml/archtun.1.wrl"
        bboxCenter -44148.000000 57399.035156 -531126.250000
        bboxSize 75800.000000 45578.054688 14878.187500
# the first of the WWWInlined objects. Note that it is also a
# WWWAnchor point, and that the actual object resides on a
# different server
    }
   }
  }
  Separator {
   WWWAnchor {
    name "http://bug.village.virginia.edu/vrml=3897"
    WWWInline {
      name
"http://jefferson.village.virginia.edu/wax/media/vrml/archtun.2.wrl"
        bboxCenter -44148.000000 57398.898438 -568568.250000
        bboxSize 75800.000000 45578.058594 14878.187500
    }
   }
  }
  Separator {
   WWWAnchor {
    name "http://bug.village.virginia.edu/vrml=3898"
    WWWInline {
      name
"http://jefferson.village.virginia.edu/wax/media/vrml/archtun.3.wrl"
        bboxCenter -44148.000000 57398.753906 -607612.250000
        bboxSize 75800.000000 45578.054688 14878.187500
    }
   }
  }
  Separator {
   WWWAnchor {
    name "http://bug.village.virginia.edu/vrml=3933"
    WWWInline {
```

```
      name
"http://jefferson.village.virginia.edu/wax/media/vrml/archtun.4.wrl"
        bboxCenter -44148.000000 57398.617188 -645054.250000
        bboxSize 75800.000000 45578.050781 14878.187500
    }
   }
  }
  Separator {
   WWWAnchor {
    name "http://bug.village.virginia.edu/vrml=3934"
    WWWInline {
      name
"http://jefferson.village.virginia.edu/wax/media/vrml/archtun.5.wrl"
        bboxCenter -44148.000000 57398.472656 -683758.250000
        bboxSize 75800.000000 45578.054688 14878.187500
    }
   }
  }
  Separator {
   WWWAnchor {
    name "http://bug.village.virginia.edu/vrml=3935"
    WWWInline {
      name
"http://jefferson.village.virginia.edu/wax/media/vrml/archtun.6.wrl"
        bboxCenter -44148.000000 57398.335938 -721200.250000
        bboxSize 75800.000000 45578.050781 14878.187500
    }
   }
  }
  Separator {
   WWWAnchor {
    name "http://bug.village.virginia.edu/vrml=3936"
    WWWInline {
      name
"http://jefferson.village.virginia.edu/wax/media/vrml/archtun.7.wrl"
```

```
          bboxCenter -44148.000000 57398.191406 -760244.250000
          bboxSize 75800.000000 45578.054688 14878.187500
      }
    }
  }
  Separator {
   WWWAnchor {
    name "http://bug.village.virginia.edu/vrml=3937"
    WWWInline {
      name
"http://jefferson.village.virginia.edu/wax/media/vrml/archtun.8.wrl"
       bboxCenter -44148.000000 57398.050781 -797686.250000
       bboxSize 75800.000000 45578.054688 14878.187500
     }
    }
   }
 }
  Separator {
  Translation { translation -44148 57398 -664406  }
  Rotation { rotation 0.209572 0.456594 -0.864639  1.62061}
  Scale { scaleFactor 281438 281438 281438 }
Separator {
  Material { diffuseColor   .6 .6 .8 }
  Scale { scaleFactor   1.8 1.8 1.8 }
  Translation { translation   0 0.3 0 }
# with the preceding, we've changed the material, rotation,
# translation and scale for the following nodes
    WWWAnchor {
       name "http://bug.village.virginia.edu/vrml=3743"
       Separator {
          Transform {
             translation 0 -.08 0
             scaleFactor 0.04 .02 .04
             rotation 1 0 0 3.14
          }
          Cone {}
      }
   }
```

```
WWWAnchor {
    name "http://bug.village.virginia.edu/vrml=11023"
    Separator {
        Transform {
            translation 0 .08 0
            scaleFactor 0.04 .02 .04
        }
        Cone {}
    }
}
}
    }
}
```

Obviously, the value of every WWWInline and WWWAnchor node can be modified each time the file is requested, but the same kind of tweaking could also be done with which Child, Rotation, Material, and other nodes as well. Essentially, everywhere you see a value (number or string) you could conceivably modify it programmatically to achieve any desired effect.

The way these VRML scenes are delivered to the user is also quite clever. Using their custom HTTP server allows WAXweb to simultaneously serve both an HTML document and the VRML node. Since almost all VRML viewers are helper applications, this means that users will receive a new page on their Web browser, and see a new VRML scene at nearly the same time.

If a user specifies a preference for VRML components from WAXweb, a VRML-based navigation tool is displayed along with the narrative. This works perfectly on an SGI machine running Netscape and WebSpace, as the image supplied by Blair indicates in Figure 7-6.

WAXweb: What Does It Mean?

Meyer, Blair, and D. Brookshire Conner, in a paper entitled "WAXweb: Toward Dynamic MOO-based VRML," admit that VRML is not very well equipped for what most people would imagine as a 3-D representation of a MUD or MOO. WAXweb is unusual in that it does not include a great deal of 3-D navigation or user interaction mediated by 3-D scenes.

Most MUD or MOO applications require more spatialized operations, like manipulating objects within a scene or interacting with other users

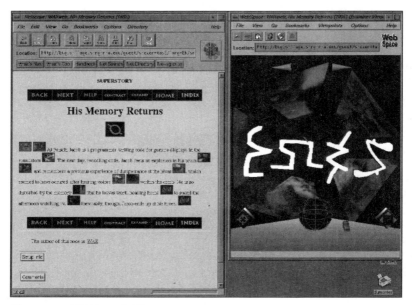

Figure 7-6: WAXweb's VRML navigation tool.

within a scene. Likewise most virtual interactions would also require programmed behaviors for objects and other capabilities not currently supported in VRML.

Furthermore, the issue of scalability is tricky once you begin looking at VRML as a means for delivering complex worlds to many users simultaneously. VRML's design centers around relatively slow delivery of text streams, to be accessible to the widest number of platforms. This puts limits on the complexity of a networked world.

In addition, the difficulty of multihoming a site puts real limits on the number of concurrent connections any VRML site can serve. Finally, the relative simplicity of VRML client software restricts the amount of work that can be offloaded from the server to the client.

Even so, it must be acknowledged that in its role as a research project, WAXweb has done a spectacular job of breaking new ground. The convergence of MOOs and VRML is nothing short of revolutionary. As Blair points out, the fact that hypertext is a framework for virtual reality which is, in turn, the navigation tool for the hypertext is ironic. A few short years ago the two disciplines seemed to diverge completely; now they hold each other up.

Blair sees the long-range relevance of WAXweb as a kind of test case for grassroots, interactive television delivered via the Web. Blair acknowledges the Internet's current shortcomings, especially when it comes to delivering continuous streams of video data. But with WAXweb Blair believes his team has created a system with more scalability, interactivity, and flexibility than most if not all of the large-scale, expensive pilot projects in interactive television.

In fact, Blair believes that we already have the mythical 500 channels today, albeit in an embryonic state, on the Internet. We are inclined to agree. The comparison Blair offers is that WAXweb, with one order of magnitude more bandwidth, would be indistinguishable from the interactivity afforded by private test networks with 50 to 100 times the bandwidth.

On the technical side, Meyer and company have accomplished great things, as well. Their implementation of dynamically constructed VRML scenes points to the future of the standard itself. In fact, the team has proposed several simple extensions to VRML 1.0 that could help significantly to address its shortcomings.

What about the WAX narrative itself? What does it mean? Is that a question that can be answered? We thought the most telling remark in Blair's paper concerned his earliest artistic influences. His two main sources of inspiration were Thomas Pynchon's *Gravity's Rainbow* and The Firesign Theater's radio sketch comedy. We thought this was telling indeed, and made WAX appear quite a bit more approachable.

Summary

We've taken a fairly comprehensive survey of the WAXweb site—from its historical roots, to its design specifications and implementations, to its technical innovations. We've looked at the specific VRML implementation for WAXweb, with its components split apart and recombined on-the-fly into whole scenes. Finally, we've discussed what WAXweb has discovered about VRML as a means for delivery, and what these findings may mean in the whole scheme of virtual reality.

Our only suggestion would be for you to visit the site and explore it for yourself. We're sure you'll be interested to see what story unfolds for you within WAXweb's many possible worlds.

## CHAPTER 8

The Virtual Vegas Online
VRML Site

Entering the City

*f*rom the moment you connect to their Web site and see the VV logo flying at you, you know that you've found a fun place to hang out online! Virtual Vegas Online from VirtualVegas Incorporated, the first VRML site we'll explore in depth, combines a variety of multimedia Web extensions with a gambling metaphor to create an online theme park (see Figure 8-1). To access their home page, point your HTML Web browser at:

```
http://www.virtualvegas.com
```

In this chapter, we'll focus on the VRML portions of the Web site, but first we'll provide an overview of the Virtual Vegas philosophy and what they have to offer.

Then we'll go into more detail about how VirtualVegas Inc. created their VRML models, and how they are currently serving them on the Internet. Next, you'll discover the ins and outs of the models themselves and how they're implemented. Finally, we'll describe the future of the Virtual Vegas VRML site.

Figure 8-1: The Virtual Vegas home page.

Sin City Online?

"Sin City" probably isn't the best choice of words to describe Virtual Vegas. There are indeed an assortment of virtual gambling games to be found in their casino—including poker, blackjack, roulette, and slot machines—but if you don't get the feeling you're doing anything wrong or illegal, it's because you aren't. Virtual Vegas is like being at an online carnival: You place bets using credits that are assigned to you after registering via an HTML form. No real money is ever involved. If you're a big winner, you get prizes that are donated by sponsors who advertise on Virtual Vegas.

Betting on the Future

There's a push in some circles to make gambling legal on the Internet. In the meantime, however, there are still lots of related issues to work out. One is that people remain reluctant to transfer money via the Internet because of questionable security. Another is that recent laws proposed in federal and state legislatures to make the Internet "safe for children" might limit the legality of online gaming.

Continued

It'll be interesting to see if the Internet's global nature will allow us to circumvent or change state and local laws regarding gambling and other regionally prohibited services. The people at Virtual Vegas think it will, and they see themselves poised to be a flagship for online casinos if gambling on the Internet becomes legal. Could this mean that in a few years marketing teams at technology companies around the globe might connect to Virtual Vegas to go to Virtual COMDEX? Egad!

Get Your Helper Apps Ready!

The ultimate goal behind Virtual Vegas is to make the Web less of a spectator sport and more interactive. The entire layout is based on a clickable imagemap of Las Vegas in cyberspace, where different buildings represent different places to visit.

These buildings link to their own HTML pages, in which you'll find other links to a variety of multimedia data and applications. The Casino allows you to play HTML forms-based gambling games, powered by CGI scripts running in the background. Stepping into the Lizard Lounge kicks off a Telnet session that connects you to a Multi-User Shared Hallucination, or MUSH. A MUSH is a "Textual Reality" zone, as they like to call it, where you can chat with other Virtual Vegas dwellers and visit rooms they've created.

In other buildings you'll find QuickTime videos, music, VRML, and other files that will put your multimedia system to the test. Along the way you'll encounter loads of beautifully rendered images of the neon-lit city after which the site is named.

Ms. Metaverse

The Ms. Metaverse Contest stands out in Virtual Vegas as a cheap and easy way to put your own multimedia project on the World Wide Web. Don't let the "Ms." designation fool you: An entrant can be practically anything that you can supply with a personality.

The guidelines for entry are simple. Your creation can be any gender or species, real or imagined, but there can be nothing illicit, and all content must be your own original work. At a minimum, the site administrators require a GIF or JPEG image file of your entrant and a short text description. They'll also accept movies, other images, sounds, text in popular formats, as well as VRML!

Visitors to the Ms. Metaverse Contest vote on which entrant they think is best, and the winner's creator wins real money, not credits. This could be a great way to get your virtual reality project launched on the Internet, as well as to finance your next project if your contestant is judged to be the sexiest being in the metaverse! To enter your project, to vote, or just to see what the fuss is all about, visit this URL:

```
http://www.virtualvegas.com/mm/mmhome.html
```

Now that you know where you can have your own VRML site in Virtual Vegas, let's see how they created theirs.

Creating the Virtual Vegas VRML Site

The staff at Virtual Vegas Online were helpful in providing information about how their site was created. They view virtual reality as the next logical step in their quest to provide an interactive experience on the World Wide Web.

They realize, however, that there are limits. These limits apply especially when it comes to the type of hardware and software most people use when accessing their site. Thus, the Virtual Vegas designers kept these limitations in mind when creating their VRML models (see Figure 8-2).

According to John Bates, the Virtual Vegas Online Director and WebMaster, the people at SGI have called their models "underwhelming." This is true if you are using an SGI Indy with a T-1 connection: In that case, you'd have processing power and bandwidth to spare. But if you're using a 486 with a 14.4Kbps modem connection to the Internet, you'll undoubtedly appreciate that their ".WRL" files are a mere 14 to 46K in size and consist of only a small number of polygons.

The Virtual Vegas team wanted to make sure that everyone could participate in the virtual reality experience. You can check out their VRML home page at:

```
http://www.virtualvegas.com/vrml/vrml.html
```

A Dedication to Open Standards

Because they want to maintain an entertaining site that the average person can use, the developers at Virtual Vegas are adamant about supporting and adhering to open standards regarding VRML and other Internet technologies. They don't want visitors to have to purchase browsers that support proprietary extensions to view their site.

Figure 8-2: The Virtual Vegas VRML home page with two of their VRML models superimposed on top.

However, Virtual Vegas says that it will make allowances when there's a browser that incorporates features that will eventually be part of an open specification, or when a browser is extremely popular. This is analogous to the early adoption of Netscape with its proposed HTML 2.0 and 3.0 standards, as well as its own HTML goodies. Many Web hosts, including Virtual Vegas, have optimized their sites for Netscape's extensions because of its popularity.

The Bad Boys of Cyberspace

On their VRML home page, Virtual Vegas offers what they call a Special Treat for the WebSpace browser. It's a model of their logo, much like the Virtual Vegas in Cyberspace model that we'll explore later. But this one has a special feature: it rotates! If you're using SGI's WebSpace, you can see it at:

```
http://www.virtualvegas.com/vrml/vv.wrl
```

Rotation is achieved using a special Open Inventor extension that isn't part of the base VRML specification—only WebSpace supports it.

> *Continued*
>
> John Bates says that when they first made this object available, it caused a flurry of responses. Most of them were people who were upset that Virtual Vegas would support a model that's not part of the open VRML standard. This, on top of the gambling theme, got Virtual Vegas the "Bad boy" title. It took quick action on their part to post a disclaimer. It states that they do support open standards, and that the rotating logo is presented only as a look at things to come in VRML. The disclaimer satisfied the masses of open standards adherents, and quickly snuffed out further flame wars!

High-End Tools

As with their images of the virtual city on their HTML pages, Virtual Vegas used SGI Indy machines to create 3-D models. The application they used is called Alias Studio, part of a high-end suite of 2-D and 3-D visualization software from Alias Research (recently acquired by Silicon Graphics). For more information about Alias software consult this URL:

```
http://www.alias.com
```

The 3-D models created in Alias were then converted into Open Inventor format using a second tool called AliasToIv. The Open Inventor format, as you may remember, is a precursor to VRML. Once this transformation was complete, it took only minor tweaking of the final output to make it fully VRML 1.0 compliant.

Vegas Wasn't Built in a Day

The Virtual Vegas VRML models were created by the Electromedia development team that includes Mike Donahue and Andrew Orloff. Andrew told us that it took them one whole weekend to create the models for the VRML page. They found it pretty easy but as we'll see, there were still some difficulties.

Simple models needed

The primary problem lay in the logistics of creating a model that could be rendered easily with a typical processor, such as a 486 PC, yet still be recognizable and interesting. Andrew and Mike considered this imperative to make their site accessible to anyone, with any type of equipment and VRML browser.

In order to optimize a scene in VRML, you must render something with the least possible number of polygons. Unfortunately, this isn't a setting that's available from a design tool today. You just have to create the model and decide whether or not it's acceptable. Inevitably, this leads to serious investments in trial-and-error graphics design!

Viewing between formats

Another problem they faced involved switching views from Alias to VRML. No matter what kind of tool they used, the model's appearance in one type of format never quite matched its appearance in the other. They found differences in color, texture, and object placement. They had to learn how to compensate for this when creating the original model, and understand what alterations would ultimately be necessary to correct any discrepancies.

It's a quandary also faced by graphic artists when taking a graphic design from its software visualization to the printed page. There are differences between multiple on-screen display models that are no less dramatic than the difference between electronic displays and ink on paper, as the Virtual Vegas design team quickly learned.

The Virtual Vegas VRML Models

Virtual Vegas in Cyberspace

From the Virtual Vegas VRML home page you can link to their rendition of Virtual Vegas in Cyberspace. Before you conjure up visions of towering spires, glittering with the names of hotels and celebrities, stretched out across a digital cityscape, let us warn you: It's actually a model of the Virtual Vegas logo. You can see it in Figure 8-3 or using a VRML browser:

```
http://www.virtualvegas.com/vrml/vvlink2.wrl
```

Virtual Vegas in Cyberspace is only around 17K in size, which makes it easy to transfer over any connection. Once your VRML browser has it loaded, you'll also find it easy to manipulate because it's constructed of only a few polygons. This object embodies the phrase "simple yet elegant."

Written in cyberspeak

Don't expect to easily comprehend the source code in any Virtual Vegas ".WRL" files. You'll find yourself going insane as you wade through a quagmire of strangely-labeled points and vectors. There are no familiar

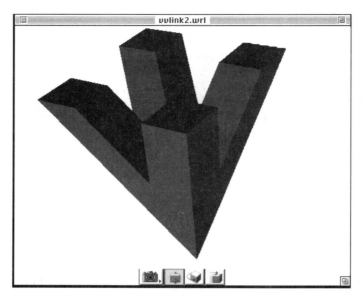

Figure 8-3: A VRML model of Virtual Vegas in Cyberspace.

words, nor guideposts along the way, to clue you in as to what's being drawn where.

You'll quickly realize that their VRML source wasn't written by hand, but was interpolated from a file generated from a 3-D modeling package using a computerized conversion tool. This is evident when you don't see descriptive labels for their nodes, such as vvlogo, but rather, more ambiguous names like node281.

Here's a sample, drawn from "VVLINK2.WRL":

```
DEF node281 Separator {
    Transform {
        translation   0 5.80595 0
        rotation    -0.57735 -0.57735 -0.57735   2.0944
    }
    DEF Polyset12 Separator {
        Transform {
        rotation    0 0 -1   1.5708
        }
        Separator {
        DEF DefaultShader+0 Material {
            ambientColor     0 0.430052 0.00891299
```

```
        diffuseColor      0 0.430052 0.00891299
        emissiveColor     0 0 0
        shininess         0
        transparency      0
    }
    Normal {
        vector    [ 0.004301 -0.933438   0.358713,
                    0.004301 -0.933438   0.358713,
                    0.621933 -0.621932   0.475816,
                    0.621933 -0.621932   0.475816,
                    0.933438 -0.00430034 0.358713,
                    0.933438 -0.00430034 0.358713 ]
    }
```

Simple enough, right? Well, it's obvious to any VRML 1.0 compliant browser, anyway!

You might recall from Chapters 2 and 3 what many of these VRML commands mean. First, a group Separator node called node281 is defined. In the Transform structure, the browser is then told that the node's initial position will be 5.80595 units up the y-axis using the *translate* statement.

In the same structure, the *rotation* statement rotates the node 2.0944 radians about an axis with an endpoint located -0.57735 units along the x-, y-, and z-axes. Then a child of node281 is created called Polyset12, which starts in a position where it's rotated 1.5708 radians along the z-axis.

Next the Material used to make the node is characterized. Because *ambientColor* and *diffuseColor* are the same, and *emissiveColor, shininess,* and *transparency* are all null, it is undoubtedly a rather flat object, with no luminescence or sheen of its own. Finally, a Normal node is defined, which contains a *vector* set. This set of 3-D vectors is defined to be used subsequently in the model, any number of times.

As you know, any child node under the group node node281 that's included within the final close-bracket delimiter is governed by its definition, light sources, textures, and other environmental definitions.

One feature that Virtual Vegas in Cyberspace does employ explicitly and effectively is the WWWAnchor tag, which happens to point to the next VRML model that we'll explore.

The Virtual Slot Machine

The Virtual Slot Machine is a more complex model than Virtual Vegas in Cyberspace, because it uses a greater variety of colors and more polygons. It's depicted in Figure 8-4, and available for rendering at the following URL:

```
http://www.virtualvegas.com/vrml/slot.wrl
```

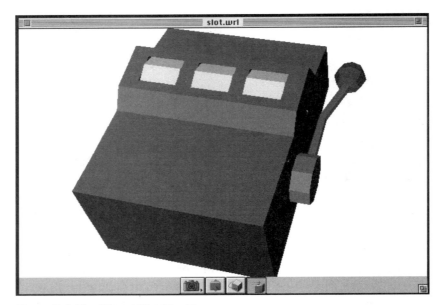

Figure 8-4: The Virtual Slot Machine.

The ".WRL" file for the Virtual Slot Machine is a relatively small 50K, which makes it a fast transfer even with a 14.4Kbps modem. Its simple composition also makes it quick to render on most any machine type that's capable of supporting a VRML browser.

Interface to Netscape

The Virtual Slot Machine gives us a picture of things to come from Virtual Vegas. It's their first foray into entertainment-oriented interactive virtual reality on their Web site.

The entire slot machine is a link back to HTML pages on the VV Web site (see Figure 8-5). Specifically, it links back to the slot machine pages

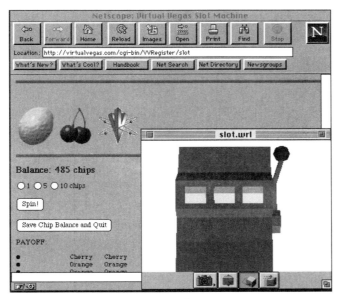

Figure 8-5: The Virtual Slot Machine VRML Model superimposed upon the HTML form for the Casino Slots page.

in their casino, where you can play CGI-driven virtual slots! Here's the actual call and URL they use:

```
WWWAnchor {

    name "http://virtualvegas.com/LOGIN/slotcash.html"

}
```

Of course, the entire slot machine node is included within the WWWAnchor tag, so that anywhere you click on the model will take you to the HTML page.

Andrew Orloff of Virtual Vegas says that he believes there are very few people incorporating this type of interaction between HTML and VRML in their Web sites.

A peek inside

Just so you don't think that VRML models are always completely solid, we'll take a look inside the Virtual Slot Machine by removing a side panel, as shown in Figure 8-6. (Don't try this at home, folks!)

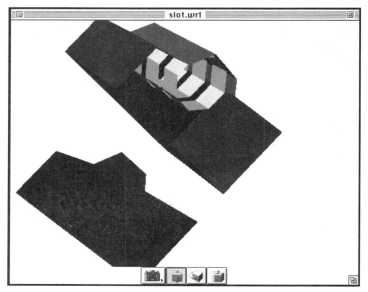

Figure 8-6: The Virtual Slot Machine VRML model with a side panel removed.

As you can see, the Virtual Slot Machine is actually hollow. Even more interesting are the spinners, which supply the cherries, lemons, bars, and other items for the slot machine's display. These spinners aren't just cosmetic panels lying on the face plate of the slot machine; they're actually 3-D wheels *inside* it! This makes the Virtual Slot Machine not just a mockup that looks good from a handful of angles, but a virtual model for the real thing!

These 3-D spinner wheels also hint at the functionality that's in the maturing VRML standard. Someday soon this specification will be expanded to add rotation and object-to-object interaction. When this takes effect, code could be added to the Virtual Slot Machine to make the wheels spin whenever the lever is clicked almost like a real slot machine.

More cyberspeak

Like "VVLINK2.WRL", the VRML code in "SLOT.WRL" is converted from Alias format to Open Inventor using AliasToIv. Therefore, it uses the same type of cryptic node designators as the former example.

Let's take a look at a recognizable object in the scene: the ball at the end of the lever. Here's part of the source code for this object:

```
DEF sphere2 Separator {
    Transform {
        translation   -0.331174 6.47335 3.48107
        scaleFactor   1.94679 1.94679 1.94679
    }
    Separator {
        DEF Shader4 Material {
        ambientColor   1 0 0
        diffuseColor   1 0 0
        emissiveColor  0 0 0
        shininess      0
        transparency   0
        }
```

First, a node called sphere2 is defined. This is not the same as the shape node Sphere, that requires only a radius. This node is like any other Separator node structure, which needs vectors to define itself. Most of the commands in the code shown above were also in the code we showed you from "VVLINK2.WRL", with the exception of *scaleFactor*.

Future Directions

Virtual Vegas has every intention of following the VRML standard as it matures and including new features in future VRML development. They see VRML as a natural extension of their entertainment atmosphere, and will no doubt stress interactivity among the people who enter their virtual world. The "textual reality" of their Lizard Lounge will extend into virtual reality, so that the rooms will have walls and furnishings. Instead of clicking on the slot machine lever, you'll actually pull it and watch the spinners whirl!

Summary

In this chapter, we've taken a lightning tour of an online rendition of Sin City. Today the Virtual Vegas site might seem simple, but someday it will be a fully realized elaborate world. The site in our next chapter is already taking steps toward this level of complexity. It's exciting to imagine the thrills our computers may bring us in future generations of software.

CHAPTER 9

Virtually
There...

Introduction

*d*uring our survey of the flourishing VRML sites that are popping into existence every day, we came across the ARC Media Festival site, which has a lovely five-story building fully rendered in VRML, complete with Web links to related sites. The Festival site itself mirrored the actual Festival's collection of artworks in a variety of forms, housing a store of almost everything that one can do with emerging interactive art forms.

Although we visited other areas and they embodied a good deal of interesting media-related information, we restricted our scope to the VRML scenes in the Variety Arts Center, an historic building located in Los Angeles.

Started as a large project to collect the capabilities of many different people in the media industry, the main focus of the ARC project is to explore the world of participatory media through exploration and total immersion. The 1995 Arc Gallery is a collection of many different works from their annual international competition.

The projects chosen for this year's exhibition illustrate the growth of interactive media by giving contributors an opportunity to explore approaches to art that include interactive television, movies. and CD-ROMs. There are also more traditional computer-focused projects, including a digital life exhibit, a digital intelligence exhibit, and a redesign of the human interface for networked computers. This is the niche occupied by the VRML project.

In this chapter, we'll explore the many facets of what it took to turn the physical Variety Arts Center into a virtual tour available in cyberspace. We will interview some the participants, detail the hardware and software used during the development cycle, and walk with them as they create a VRML scene. Finally, we'll pick their brains for some of the more obscure but helpful tips and tricks they discovered during this project's creation and implementation.

But first, let's visit the Interactive Media Festival, to get a feel for what all the hubbub is about.

ARC: An Interactive Media Festival

The Variety Arts Center in Los Angeles was chosen for the site of the ARC Media Festival in 1995. Hence, it is a perfect choice for an ambitious VRML model that can best exemplify the power and breadth of what Virtual Reality can deliver.

The Center itself is a fantastic building constructed in 1891. It sports a nightclub, a cabaret theater, a full bar with an adjoining restaurant, and remarkably enough, a 1,000-seat theater. Architecturally, the building is quite a resource for would-be VRML modelers: It offers high ceilings, sculpted balconies, and scrollwork pillars as a source of inspiration and images. By capturing just a teaspoon of the building's character and essence, those involved in the VRML project could be assured of immediate success. And now, on to the magic...

The Arc VRML Site details the phases of construction, the programmers, sponsors, and actual VRML pages. If you have a VRML browser, you can see it in all its glory:

```
http://www.arc.org/vrml/index.html
```

The Designers and Managers

In their own words: "Arc is a collection of lots of things. There's the Staff, the Jury, the Artists, the friends and family, the essential and supporting people that help us without any of the recognition they deserve, and the bodies gathered from all over the U.S., but mostly the San Francisco Bay Area."

Because the Arc project is more of a generic Interactive Media Festival and not merely a VRML-only exposition, we'll point out that the 1995 winners featured in the following URL are indeed leaders in their respective fields:

```
http://www.arc.org/gallery95/
```

And Now to the Jury...

The selections in The Gallery were chosen by a wide range of people (affectionately termed "The Jury"). The Jury consists of art critics, professors, and industry visionaries, from all walks of life and from every corner of the globe. It included representatives from the Japanese, Finnish, American, and Australian cultures, all with their own ideas and angles to offer. Jurors were selected for their highly respected standing in society, and for their ability to overlook the seductive appeal of "technology for technology's sake."

The Judging of the Festival: Taken from the Arc Home Page

Whereas the previously separate categories of the arts, entertainment, business, and technology are in many ways converging, criteria for evaluating interactivity are still emergent. Therefore, the Festival Jury has been chosen for its diversity and the depth and range of its experience. Explicitly, the Jury will explore its fields of interest in search of creative works expressing new models of behavior, consciousness, and culture: open systems—involving dispersed authorship, networks, artificial life, intelligent environments, etc.; self-contained forms—in which the authorship of the work is clearly identified, such as disc-based media and installations that offer a variety of interfaces, navigational pathways, databases, etc.; significant developments in the creative uses of the technological infrastructure.

Works selected for the Festival will be compelling and innovative in concept and execution. Evaluation will be on the basis of:

- The strength of realization of concept.
- The transformative power of the work.
- The ability of the participant to affect the performance of the work.
- The quality of feedback in the structure of the work.

> **Continued**
>
> The Festival will be global in scope and in aspirations. It is the ambition of the Festival to contribute to the advancement of interactive media as an integrative force in the confluence of cultural and economic forces which are determining the future.

To find out who's serving on the ARC's Jury, turn your browser to this Web page:

```
http://www.arc.org/who/jury95.html
```

A Retrospective: The Interactive Media Festival

The Interactive Media Festival was begun as an exchange of multimedia ideas and technologies; as an incubator of sorts intended to explore the futures of video, audio, and interfaces, and where these technologies were headed.

In 1993, Motorola, Inc. agreed to be the Festival's first large sponsor, thereby thrusting industry giants onto the scene and supporting the notion that they weren't turning a tin ear to development in the interactive media milieu. In 1994, things got really busy when the Festival targeted all forms of media interactivity. It was during this year that the thought originated of having a large pool of experienced people nominate the works for the Festival, coupled with a smaller group of hand-selected jurors, to pick through the nominations for the truly outstanding entries.

The criteria used for choosing worthy entries include: educational value, entertainment value, aesthetic design, success in meeting design goals, and interactivity itself. Since these criteria also sound like good measuring sticks to apply to Web and VRML sites, it seems only natural that these new technologies have been fully adopted by the festival.

The Players

Now that we've described the Festival and where the treadmill of this project is taking us, let's check out the participants who made it all possible. The 25 people who did the bulk of the work were loosely divided into two major groups: the Modeling and Linking Crüe, and the Video Crüe. Most of them met in cyberspace at the WELL (Whole Earth 'Lectronic Link Internet Chat Area/Lounge, *http://www.well.com/*).

The Modeling and Linking Crüe was organized mostly from San Francisco, and the Video Crüe hailed primarily from Los Angeles. For completeness sake, we've have included the names of all the superb coders and graphics designers whose input was invaluable to us in our quest for information about this project, among other things:

The Modeling and Linking Crüe

Thomas Caleshu	Michael Gerstein	Todd Goldenbaum
Adam Gould	Michael Gough	Jeffrey Gray
Ian Kallen	Vojislav Lalich-Petrich	David Lewis
Annette Loudon	Mark S. Meadows	Steven Piasecki
Jim Race	James Waldrop	

The Video Crüe

Gavin Doughtie	Daniel R. Kegel	Jeannine Parker
Richard G. Gilligan	Jeff Sherwood	John Aleck Mellon
Michael Boehm	Steve Arbuss	Karlos Nazarian

The people involved in this project willingly volunteered their own time, and coupled with the generous donations from some large sponsors, made the project coalesce. Much of the effort was directed by Mark Meadows, who did an exemplary job of organizing and completing the project on time.

Now let's take a tour and see what this extraordinary team accomplished.

A Look at the Design

In speaking with Mark Meadows, WebMaster of the ARC site, as well as a few of the VRML code-hounds, we got a good description of the tools used to render the Variety Arts Center.

At the time the project was begun, in April, 1995, there were only a scant few VRML applications actually running on anything other than SGI machines. As a result, the majority of the work was done with Macintosh computers running a variety of modeling software packages, all of which were ultimately transformed into their final VRML formats using some sophisticated translation utilities.

The bulk of the work was done with FormZ, a high-powered, high-class application that produces very good images of 3-D models. 3D-Studio and StrataStudioPro were used in a similar capacity for their modeling and rendering capabilities.

Because each of these applications did *not* support VRML as an option for saving these files, the common interchange file type known as *DXF* emerged as the logical choice. Although DXF did present some trouble, the group managed to get things into a digestible format for conversion, then for viewing, with a couple of scripts that members of the team created on-the-fly. We'll take a look at them later in this chapter, but first let's review the tools that the team used.

The Implementation in Action

In this section, we'll examine the authoring tools used to create scenes and images, the tools used to convert them to standard formats (and ultimately, to VRML), and the proofing tools used to check the resulting virtual worlds that the designers wanted to build. Along the way, we think you'll learn as much from this talented team as we did, as we explore what they used to create the 1995 ARC environment.

You'll notice that all of these applications are the same popular ones that you could find on the shelf today in a local computer store, or through a mail-order distributor. Although they weren't specifically designed for VRML output, they're all great modeling and rendering applications, which the Arc folks wholeheartedly believe to be capable of performing that duty.

Authoring Tools

FormZ by AutoDesSys was the most favored application because it was used for the gross architecture modeling, and the architect who was part of the team preferred it above other available options.

AutoCAD, a product of AutoDesk, was used to proof and double-check the models. Since it is a very close companion to 3DStudio (also by AutoDesk), the team could use it to check file conversions after the fact (a very common procedure).

Strata StudioPro, created and distributed by Strata Inc., was used for modeling those highly specific, high-resolution objects that would need to be placed into the VRML scenes. FormZ was used to import the Strata Files where they would be assembled, after which they would be exported to 3DStudio for a final version.

3DStudio was warmly praised by everyone who was involved with coding the Arc project. One of the best tips that we came away with from their design procedure was that 3DStudio was a great all-in-one product. There was little need to keep exporting, converting, and re-exporting files across several programs because, as they learned over time, 3DStudio can do it all.

Converters

During the entire production cycle, the Arc team needed to convert a lot of files into a common format so that they could ultimately produce VRML scenes for their Web site. This is no easy task, let us assure you, especially in the rarefied realm of 3-D graphics.

Unless you want to code VRML by hand (which we wouldn't recommend other than as a learning exercise) the best approach is to use an application for modeling that you already know, save the file as DXF, then convert it to Inventor (IV) format. From Inventor it's fairly trivial going to VRML, since VRML's genesis was based on the Open Inventor file format, both closely linked to Silicon Graphics. Table 9-1 lists the handful of converters that the Arc development engineers used to make their magic, with a brief description of each one.

Table 9-1: The Converters Used in the Arc VRML Project*

CONVERTER	DESCRIPTION
Transporter	With over 140 different flavors of DXF, this was a lifesaver that could handle practically anything.
dxfToIv	Takes DXF files and converts them into Open Inventor Format.
3dsToIv	Takes 3DStudio files and converts them into Open Inventor Format.
IvToVRML	Converts Inventor files directly into VRML.

*All of these tools are available at the SGI Web site at:

`http://www.sgi.com/Technology/Inventor.html`

Proofing Tools

When checking their work after the various translations, the Arc team would typically use either WebSpace for the SGI platform, a new version for Windows NT, or SceneViewer. In our browsing of the Arc Web site, we were unable to get most of our public-domain-obtained clients to display their scenes in as high a level of detail or realism as an SGI WebSpace application could provide. Most of our images looked something like the one featured in Figure 9-1, taken from a Mac running MacX, against a Sun Sparc 2 running VRWeb for Sun with the MESA libraries.

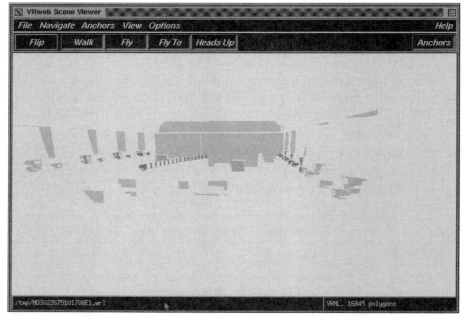

Figure 9-1: The 4th floor of the Variety Arts Center seen by VRWeb.

It's quite evident that the image was very close to its inspiration, and only needed some work with this specific viewer to fix the missing light source problems, and to repair the mismatched texture mapping we noticed. Since the VRML specification is still in its infancy, little annoyances like this are inevitable. To show that the scene was still intact and to illustrate its sheer complexity, take a look at Figure 9-2, where we show the wireframe model for the same scene. Pretty busy, eh?

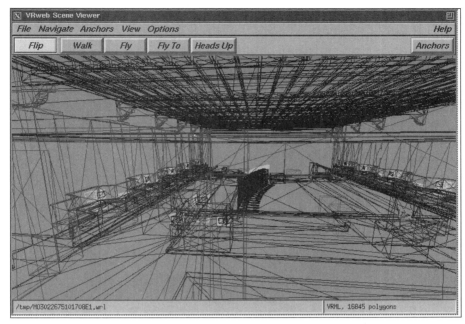

Figure 9-2: The 4th floor of the Variety Arts Center in Wire Outline.

Finally, Figure 9-3 paints a picture of what the scene would look like if it were viewed exactly as it should appear. Notice we had to use WebSpace to get the full effect. Someday soon, any VRML viewer should be able to sketch that same view without any observable discrepancies.

Figure 9-3: The 4th floor of the Variety Arts Center à la WebSpace.

To get an idea of what the Variety Arts Center looks like as it actually stands in downtown Los Angeles, check out Figures 9-4 and 9-5. Both depict the size and scope of what the VRML coders faced. The development of the site involved lots of picture-taking, for which the Video Crüe was mainly responsible.

Figure 9-4: A real photo of the Variety Arts Center.

Figure 9-5: Another real photo of the Variety Arts Center.

These photographs were given to the Arc's resident architect, who used FormZ to sculpt large structural models. Smaller objects were modeled using either 3DStudio or Strata, and were later merged into the scene using translation utilities or scripts that the team wrote expressly for that purpose.

All in all, the team had quite a good system going, especially considering that it involved two collections of people in two different cities. In Figure 9-6, you'll see what one of the rough models of the building looks like, without the complex smaller objects or texture mappings in place.

Figure 9-6: Architectural model of the 1st floor of Variety Arts.

Compare Figure 9-7 with Figures 9-1 through 9-3. Figure 9-7 depicts the same scene from a slightly askew angle, without the benefit of lighting, objects, or other cluttering obstructions. It shows what a VRML model of a room without frills can look like before it has been dressed up.

Cool Tools

To help the Arc team get the show on the road, some helpful tools were created to quickly Webify some of the more complex scenes (i.e., make them palatable to retrieve via the Web). The final output that is produced by some of the back-and-forth translators, or directly from one of the modeling programs may be quite large, and thus cumbersome and expensive to transfer repeatedly over the Web.

Generally it's common to try and keep graphics, even those as meaty as VRML scenes, down to 100-200K in size. VRML, like its mother Open Inventor, can be wickedly precise in describing the mathematics of an object to the point of actually making it too big to handle in some cases.

Figure 9-7: The 4th floor in Simple (compare to Figures 9-1 through 9-3).

One of the team members, James Waldrop, wrote a nice little Perl script that cut the precision down to two digits and zeroed out ridiculously small numbers expressed in scientific notation (such as 1.002374e-23). By using this script to trim the Arc files, some of the larger ones were actually chopped in half, resulting in faster, easier renders.

The final interesting thing we discovered on the Arc site was a public service DXF-to-VRML converter box for anyone to use. Organic Online has been gracious enough to sponsor the service, detailed exactly as we found it in the next paragraphs:

> As a public service to the VRML community, Organic Online is providing a totally public DXF to VRML conversion service. Here's how it works:
>
> 1. Upload your DXF files to *ftp.organic.com*, in the directory */incoming/dxf*. Obviously, you need to be using an FTP client that can upload files. These directories are "blind" directories, so

you won't be able to see your files or anyone elses's — if you get a "permission denied" rename your file.

2. Wait 1 hour. Every hour a cron job converts any files it finds there and moves it to the web server. It may take a little longer to actually propagate to our web server, so please be patient and try again in a few hours if you don't get it the first time.

3. Access *http://www.organic.com/vrml/*, and append to the URL the name of the file, plus a .wrl. So, if you uploaded a file called "boat", you would access the URL *http://www.organic.com/vrml/boat.wrl*. The file will be served with the MIME type of *x-world/x-vrml*, so it will either prompt you to save it or send it to Webspace. If the file is completely blank, it meant that "DxfToIv" refused to recongize it as a valid DXF file, so try changing something in the file and reupload it.

The reason these files are not currently public is so that people can develop their scenes in semi-privacy - if you have something you'd like to make public, let me know and I will move it to the public directory. I will be occasionally deleting old .wrl files as space requirements increase, so remember to download it and save it as soon as possible.

The conversion is done using DxfToIv and IvToVRML, two tools written for the SGI platform. A tremendous amount of appreciation goes to SGI for creating these tools and for boostering the VRML project. Make sure it is a valid DXF file! They usually have a string of words or numbers separated by single carriage returns.

—*Brian Behlendorf, brian@organic.com.*

Access to this powerful tool and to the powerful CPU it runs on are real boons for VRML coders. They help to lower the hurdles that can make your first VRML project intimidating, and will hopefully encourage more efforts as ambitious as the Arc VRML project. Cheers to Organic Online!

A Virtual Walkthrough of the Process

The 25 or so people on the project team worked extremely hard, mostly at the eleventh hour, to mass produce the huge amounts of VRML required to describe a building the size and scope of the Variety Arts Center. They followed a neat little process for development: it's always nice to have a list of steps to drive you to your goal, and it looks like they found quite a winner. While their method may not be the most straightforward, it got the job done. That's why we present it here.

Here's How They Did It

The recipe is in their own words:

1. Model objects in object modeling application.
2. Model architecture in architecture program.
3. Import objects as DXF and export as DXF.
4. Assign layers that will link.
5. Export/save faces as 3-D polylines or 3-D faces.
6. Open file in 3D Studio.
7. Add colors and lighting.
8. Translate from 3D Studio to IV.
9. Translate from IV to VRML.
10. Add link and viewpoints to the finished scene.
11. Chill and serve (probably the most important step).

Summary

We hope you've enjoyed this tour of the Los Angeles Variety Arts Center. We tried to explicate what it took to build, render, capture, and contain it.

We discussed the Arc project in general with a particular focus on the VRML project undertaken this year. The objective was to render a complete, real building in VRML, and to make the resulting scenes accessible through the WWW. We hope that learning about their experiences and processes will aid you in developing your own VRML sites. We also hope that knowing some of the pitfalls encountered by the designers will help you to avoid them in your work. Finally, we hope to see your VRML site when you have it done!

In the next chapter, we'll ask you to put your futurist's goggles on, as we conclude the book with a series of far-out projects about the future of VRML, and where this technology could take us.

The Future of
VRML

What about Today?

*W*ith only a 1.0 version available, VRML is still in its infancy. Today, we'd have to say that while VRML certainly offers interesting capabilities, its most useful applications still remain just beyond the horizon.

As this future is realized, what we call VRML today may very well be called something else entirely. Nevertheless, it's clear from VRML's enthusiastic reception on the Web that there's a powerful demand for three-dimensional representations of data, and an attendant ability to interact with more realistic "virtual spaces."

As we begin to close out this investigation of VRML, the real questions we'd like to tackle are:

- What's VRML good for today?
- What are VRML's most serious limitations?

These are the topics for the two sections that follow.

What's VRML Good for Today?

The short and flippant answer to this question, despite the heroic efforts of its inventors and the thousands of hours that have gone into programming existing VRML applications, is unfortunately: "not much." In its present form, VRML is limited to applications for viewing 3-D spaces. Currently, there's no capability to support interaction between multiple users, nor even between users and their environment, except for limited displays (like the Virtual Vegas Slot Machine covered in Chapter 8).

Nevertheless, even within this limited functionality, today's implementation of VRML offers interesting potential applications. As illustrated by the examples in the three preceding chapters, VRML does permit interesting capability for "architectural walkthroughs" of virtual spaces.

In addition to the obvious entertainment possibilities this affords, VRML could deliver what we'll call "ecologically sensitive" virtual tours. For example, the caves at Altamira in Spain contain some of the richest examples of Paleolithic art ever discovered. But the light that's so necessary for viewing these paintings, along with the carbon dioxide in visitors' exhalations, are causing these paintings to deteriorate to the point where only a limited number of researchers are allowed access to the caves.

Existing photographs could be combined to create a three-dimensional texture map of the caves and a realistic model of the artwork could be rendered using VRML. This model could be visited millions of times over without doing any further damage to the original site. The same is true for other sensitive archaeological and architectural treasures—once a virtual model has been built, visitors can experience these sites online rather than in situ. Not only will this help to preserve the originals, it will make them more accessible than ever before!

Likewise, the efforts at the National Center for Supercomputing Applications (NCSA) to model cosmological objects point to other useful applications for today's VRML. This site includes a "Spacetime Diagram for the Collision of 2 Black Holes" which is also whimsically known as a "Pair of Pants" figure because that's what it most closely resembles. It features a number of figures of Teukolsky waves evolved using NCSA's 3-D General Relativity Code, and some interesting models of gas surrounding a galaxy cluster. For a look at this site, visit either of the following URLs:

```
http://jean-luc.ncsa.uiuc.edu/Viz/VRML/
http://www.ncsa.uiuc.edu/General/VRML/
```

Apparently, VRML is well-suited for visualizing complex mathematical functions and relationships, and is proving to be a useful teaching tool for math-intensive areas of study and research. We expect that disciplines like genetics, molecular biology, particle physics, and chemistry will benefit from using VRML as a teaching tool. In fact, VRML appears to offer significant educational ability for any kind of information that benefits from visualization and observation.

Another area where VRML's current implementation can add value is in its ability to make individual objects within a scene lead the user to other HTML and VRML documents when clicked (like clickable image maps in two-dimensional HTML). This promises to support three-dimensional metaphors for user interfaces that could be both more powerful and more interesting than current technologies. The WAX site profiled in Chapter 7 acts like an interface to an oblique game and serves as a good example of the kinds of navigation and interaction such an interface could supply.

Likewise, much of the Virtual Vegas site discussed in Chapter 8 uses a gaming or gambling metaphor, and again demonstrates some of the possibilities inherent in VRML. Our final site survey, the ARC site, also presents a 3-D interface that allows the user to browse the contents of the Web server. Since the media and entertainment industries now outstrip the defense industries in driving the U.S. (and global) economies, we expect entertainment applications to be a driving force in the further development of VRML and related technologies.

What Are VRML's Most Serious Limitations?

Here again, the short answer is: "VRML's lack of interaction, animation, and behaviors." An even shorter answer is that VRML is fundamentally static. Even the least sophisticated user who encounters VRML for the first time can immediately recognize that it ain't no VR5!

Today, VRML supports no real interaction among users who may be simultaneously present in VRML scenes, nor even interaction between individual users and elements of a scene. In fact, since a scene graph is downloaded in its entirety to the user's machine, there is no awareness on the part of the server that a given user is "present" in the scene, nor any pre-existing ability to support the concept of being "in" a scene in the 1.0 specification. In short, a scene behaves like a single object, so that it can only be rotated and redrawn as a whole, rather than in terms of individual nodes.

Likewise, there's no animation capability in the current VRML definition. Not only must an entire scene be rendered as a single meta-object, there's no facility to move individual objects, nor to apply the kinds of regular transformations that would allow them to be animated.

Finally, there's currently no provision for what is sometimes called "object behavior" in VRML. This concept refers to the assignment of properties to objects that would define how they'd behave, whether in motion by themselves, or in combination with other objects. A good example of this property for objects of the class "ball" might be "bounciness." As we all know from real-world experience, balls made of hard rubber (like a tennis ball or Super ball) will bounce longer and higher than balls made of foam (like Nerf balls). An important part of animating 3-D worlds will depend on the description and modeling of such behavior for objects, whether they're modeled after real or imaginary things.

Fortunately, there's a great deal of research work already underway to define descriptive techniques—and corresponding implementations—to bring to life these characteristics that are currently lacking in VRML. A company called BEsoft is developing embedded behaviors within SGI Open Inventor files. This work may ultimately overlap into a future VRML draft specification. For more information on this work, see the following URL:

```
http://www.besoft.com/bef/index.html
```

Likewise, a team of talented individuals at Chicago-based VREAM, Inc. is building what they call *WIRL* (Web Interactive Reality Layer). This is a fully interactive 3-D Web browser designed for, in the words of their press release, "allowing Web users to experience virtual reality across the Internet." They also offer an authoring tool, called *VRCreator*, designed to assist in the creation of virtual worlds, to make it easier to build virtual reality environments. For more information, visit their URL:

```
http://www.vream.com/wirl/
```

Under the hood, WIRL adds the ability to script embedded behaviors into objects in a three-dimensional scene. This allows them to respond to user input in a wide variety of ways (by moving, changing shape,

IDG BOOKS WORLDWIDE REGISTRATION CARD

RETURN THIS REGISTRATION CARD FOR FREE CATALOG

Title of this book: The Internet World 60 Minute Guide To VRML

My overall rating of this book: ❏ Very good [1] ❏ Good [2] ❏ Satisfactory [3] ❏ Fair [4] ❏ Poor [5]

How I first heard about this book:

❏ Found in bookstore; name: [6]
❏ Advertisement: [8]
❏ Word of mouth; heard about book from friend, co-worker, etc.: [10]

❏ Book review: [7]
❏ Catalog: [9]
❏ Other: [11]

What I liked most about this book:

What I would change, add, delete, etc., in future editions of this book:

Other comments:

Number of computer books I purchase in a year: ❏ 1 [12] ❏ 2-5 [13] ❏ 6-10 [14] ❏ More than 10 [15]

I would characterize my computer skills as: ❏ Beginner [16] ❏ Intermediate [17] ❏ Advanced [18] ❏ Professional [19]

I use ❏ DOS [20] ❏ Windows [21] ❏ OS/2 [22] ❏ Unix [23] ❏ Macintosh [24] ❏ Other: [25]_____
(please specify)

I would be interested in new books on the following subjects:
(please check all that apply, and use the spaces provided to identify specific software)

❏ Word processing: [26]
❏ Data bases: [28]
❏ File Utilities: [30]
❏ Networking: [32]
❏ Other: [34]

❏ Spreadsheets: [27]
❏ Desktop publishing: [29]
❏ Money management: [31]
❏ Programming languages: [33]

I use a PC at (please check all that apply): ❏ home [35] ❏ work [36] ❏ school [37] ❏ other: [38] _____

The disks I prefer to use are ❏ 5.25 [39] ❏ 3.5 [40] ❏ other: [41]_____

I have a CD ROM: ❏ yes [42] ❏ no [43]

I plan to buy or upgrade computer hardware this year: ❏ yes [44] ❏ no [45]

I plan to buy or upgrade computer software this year: ❏ yes [46] ❏ no [47]

Name: _____   Business title: [48] _____   Type of Business: [49] _____

Address (❏ home [50] ❏ work [51] /Company name: _____)

Street/Suite# _____

City [52]/State [53]/Zipcode [54]: _____   Country [55] _____

❏ **I liked this book!** You may quote me by name in future
IDG Books Worldwide promotional materials.

My daytime phone number is _____

IDG BOOKS

THE WORLD OF
COMPUTER
KNOWLEDGE

 # YES!

Please keep me informed about IDG's World of Computer Knowledge.
Send me the latest IDG Books catalog.

etc.), rather than simply by acting as hyperlinks (as objects do in the current VRML implementation). WIRL also acts as a superset of VRML, fully supporting the 1.0 specification, which points toward some possibility of future integration of VRML and WIRL, or at least portions thereof.

User interaction with 3-D scenes is the focus of work underway on an extension to VRML called *VRML+*. This effort is designed to allow users to be represented by customizable entities called "Digital Actors" within a scene, where their movements are communicated to other people who are viewing the same scene. This should help to contribute to a sense of user interaction in virtual spaces, and to a heightened sense of "consensual virtual reality" (right now, virtual reality under VRML is a pretty lonely place). For more information on VRML+ see the following URL:

```
http://www.worlds.net/products/vrmlplus/index.html
```

To facilitate the delivery of virtual reality over the Web, a next-generation Web server called *Marilyn*, with built-in VRML support, is under development at Tenet Networks in Carlsbad, CA. Their stated goals are to provide:

- Application of transaction processing technology to support 10,000+ concurrent users within one or more virtual realities.
- Server side technology to support three-dimensional objects and VRML construction.
- A C++ class library for the construction of high-performance servers.

In short, this group wants to define and develop a new class of Web servers that can handle the demands placed by a large number of users sharing one or more virtual realities. While this is a challenging enterprise, it will surely help to deliver the kind of interactive virtual reality that most users are looking for (whether they know it or not). For more information on Marilyn and Tenet visit their Web site at:

```
http://www.tenet.net/html/projects.html
```

Meanwhile, Virtus Corporation in Cary, NC, is busy at work defining VRML export capabilities into their 3-D modeling and visualization software. Their acclaimed Virtus WalkThrough Pro and Virtus VR products are already designed to build and maintain 3-D virtual realities, and their goal is to make it easy to build and manage such virtual spaces as Web sites. Their claim to technological fame is their ability to let users walk through and interact with virtual spaces, which served as the foundation for the award-winning Macintosh game, The Colony. For more information on their efforts, go to:

```
http://www.virtus.com/pr.vrml.html
```

In keeping with their desire to have a finger in every technological pie, Microsoft has also staked out a large and interesting presence in virtual reality technology. Their RenderMorphics division offers a package called *The Reality Lab*, a cross-platform development environment aimed at delivering what they describe (in their own characteristically modest way) as "the world's most advanced high performance real-time software 3-D rendering library."

Microsoft's goals in this area are ambitious and well-conceived. They want to provide workstation-class, three-dimensional visualization and interaction capability for PCs, at a fraction of the current cost for such systems. Although a certain amount of hyperbole is normal for Microsoft, this product did serve as the foundation for InterVista's Worldview for Windows VRML browser (see Chapter 6), which we judged to be the best of the Windows VRML browsers headed to market right now, so it can't be all hype. For more information about what Microsoft is up to in this area, visit their Web site at:

```
http://www.gold.net/oneday/render/index.html
```

We could go on and on in reviewing exciting new areas in VRML and related 3-D viewing environments. But by now, we hope it's abundantly clear that neither VRML nor virtual reality research stops with the capabilities included in the 1.0 version of its specification. In fact, we're looking forward to significant improvements in its representational and behavioral characteristics in the next year! This expectation leads us to ask (and attempt to answer) the fundamental question about the future.

What Kinds of Applications Should You Expect to See in the Future?

While we're not 100% sure that these applications will be coded in VRML, we're pretty sure that they'll partake of much of its approach and capabilities, albeit with significant extensions. Nevertheless, we expect VRML and related development efforts to spawn a whole new class of interactive applications right away and into the foreseeable future. And, we expect it to be pretty exciting stuff, not just for entertainment, but for all kinds of practical uses, too.

For one thing, it's clear that current research is aimed at remedying the most obvious deficiencies in VRML's current implementation. Significant efforts are already underway to add animation; interaction among and between users and the scenes they occupy; and behavior to objects in a scene. The question we raised at the beginning of the chapter is hard to answer specifically (since we don't have a crystal ball, virtual or otherwise), so we'd like to restate it as: "What kind of applications will this make possible?"

For one thing, we'd certainly expect behaviors and animations for individual objects within a scene to completely revolutionize the repair and maintenance industries. Given that most mechanical, electrical, and other systems are already designed using CAD software (and hence, already available as 3-D models), we expect to see VRML (or some future extension) enable technicians to disassemble and reassemble virtual parts of motors, equipment, and vehicles to help them in working with the real thing. Since large, complex systems like trains, aircraft, and motor vehicles already incorporate large collections of paper manuals to support these tasks, VRML could make it possible for technicians to carry small portable PCs instead of huge stacks of paper to help them do their jobs.

In a similar vein, we'd expect to see the delivery of complete 3-D anatomical models to help surgeons, veterinarians, biologists, botanists, and other professionals operate on or dissect real-world analogs. Likewise, virtual reality may be able to deliver even more realistic simulations of aircraft, ships, and other expensive gear for whose operation extensive training is required, when compared to today's multimillion dollar aircraft simulators. Once digital actors can manipulate controls and objects in their environments "as if they were real," there's no reason why only the view from the windows in an aircraft simulator would have to be computer-generated; at that point, the whole thing could be virtual!

At a far finer level of detail, molecular chemists or biologists should be able to model particular compounds or organic molecules and interact with them to design new molecules or to better understand the behavior of living systems. In particular, we expect activities like gene-splicing and DNA analysis to be greatly facilitated by interacting directly with and manipulating digital models.

Likewise, data gathered by x-ray diffraction of crystals, cloud chamber observations, and other diagnostic tools for encountering the atomic and subatomic worlds could result in simulations and predictive models for developing new theories and approaches based on a newfound ability to "get small" and interact directly with these worlds.

At a cosmological level, we've seen the pioneering work at NCSA to represent gravity waves, black holes, and the behavior of galaxies. We believe that these kinds of tools and approaches will become a stock element in the astronomer's and astrophysicist's bags of tricks, as they attempt to use theories to build visualizations (and ultimately, to go the other way around, and use visualizations to build theories).

In short, we expect this kind of technology to have a sweeping impact on the way we interact with our world, from the very smallest of its components at a subatomic level, to the very largest of its structures, at the level of cosmology. It's hard to image something broader than that!

What Barriers Remain?

Given that we can conceive of these capabilities today, what prevents their immediate realization? In large part, we still lack the right kinds of software and visualization tools to support full implementation of arbitrary virtual realities. Thus, while VRML represents a significant step in creating the right toolset, there are still lots of components missing.

First among these components is a set of standards for the kinds of extensions to VRML that we've been discussing here. It's widely recognized that supporting interactivity, describing object behaviors, providing real-time object animation, and creating digital actors are all necessary to extend VRML, to make it more useful and "more real."

Although there's lots of research work underway in each of these areas, these efforts are currently disjointed. Also, none of them is directly aimed at standardization. Until the initial research and some sample implementations are complete, and an agreed-upon set of characteristics and behaviors can be developed for each area, standardization would be premature.

Yet widespread use of virtual reality won't be possible until meaningful standards can be defined and deployed. That's the inevitable paradox involved in adopting and adapting to new technologies—it's necessary to push advanced development as far and as fast as possible, but the results of such labors can only become widespread when they've settled down enough to be somewhat stable and standard.

Given the demands of re-creating a meaningful enough subset of the characteristics that make up a real world, it's also safe to say that there are still some platform limitations holding back delivery of virtual reality to the average desktop computer. Moore's Law makes it clear that ever-more capable computers are just around the corner, but the demands of virtual reality still won't be met for some time to come.

Then, too, server-side support for virtual reality is also still very much in its infancy. Aside from Tenet's work with Marilyn and WAXweb's prototype adaptation of a MOO server to serve VRML scenes, we didn't discover many meaningful efforts underway to extend server technology specifically for delivering more and better virtual reality support. This area will have to receive more attention and development effort before the size of the community that interacts via virtual reality can begin to approach that of the total online community (let alone the human community).

Despite these limitations, we see VRML as a meaningful step toward the widespread delivery of virtual reality to the average Internet user. It appears to have provoked a strong response in the developer and user communities, and has certainly raised the level of activity and interest around the phenomenon known as virtual reality. In fact, we believe that technology and interface ergonomics, coupled with decreasing costs and increasing capabilities for computing, make the movement toward virtual reality both inevitable and inexorable. There's only a huge mass of problems, details, and implementation standing in the way!

Summary

Throughout this book, we've explored VRML's current structures and capabilities, while trying to understand its motivation and technical limitations. In this chapter, we've extended our scope to speculate on what VRML could mean to the future of networking (and computing). We've extended its potential impact from subatomic worlds all the way to cosmic proportions. Hopefully, we haven't lost your enthusiasm or understanding along the way.

In closing, we'd like to leave you with an annotated list of Web sites that you can use to further extend your own studies of VRML and related phenomena and technologies. We sincerely hope that you've found our coverage herein to be useful and illuminating, and that you'll continue your investigations on your own. In an area as new and fluid as virtual reality, there's no substitute for staying current with new and emerging theories, technologies, and implementations. Our concluding list of Web resources should help you keep track of the companies, technologies, and people that are making VRML (and in large part, virtual reality) happen.

Specific Resources Worth Visiting

The Hypermail Archive for the VRML mailing list:

```
http://gopher.wired.com/arch/
```

A statement of the goals for the VRML mailing list:

```
http://boris.qub.ac.uk/vrml/concepts/listgoals.html
```

The C++ VRML library, QvLib 1.0b1:

```
http://www.eit.com/vrml/qv.html
```

The VRML FAQ is a useful source of overall information that's updated regularly:

```
http://www.oki.com/vrml/VRML_FAQ.html
```

A set of "VRML celebrity" biographies:

```
http://boris.qub.ac.uk/vrml/bios/
```

Webified minutes on Mecklermedia's VR World 95 Convention:

```
http://www.mecklerweb.com/shows/vrw95/update.htm
```

A VRML authenticator service (to test correctness and conformance to the specification):

```
http://www.geom.umn.edu/~daeron/docs/vrml.html
```

Layne Thomas's home page with his own "Home World," his *txt2wrl* source and examples, and cool tools. (We think it's just a matter of time before "Home World" replaces "Home page" as a Web concept!)

```
http://www.cs.uah.edu/~lthomas/vrml/
```

General Resources Worth Visiting

A nice set of VRML meta-meta pointers:

```
http://www.vrml.org/
```

A mega-site of VRML references, sites, and tools:

```
http://www.lightside.com/3dsite/cgi/VRML-index.html
```

Yahoo's VRML search results:

```
http://www.yahoo.com/Entertainment/Virtual_Reality/
Virtual_Reality_Modeling_Language__VRML_/
```

The San Diego Super Computing center has a great repository of VRML information:

```
http://www.sdsc.edu/vrml
```

Wired magazine's archive is a well-known clearinghouse for VRML information (includes details on joining mailing list):

```
http://vrml.wired.com
```

For information about Virtual Reality in the larger sense:

```
http://www.cs.vu.nl:80/~lgonggr/VRLinks.html
```

```
ftp://ftp.u.washington.edu/public/virtual-worlds/WWW/scivw-faq.html
```

Finally, the Stars Virtual Library is a great source about any Web-related programming issues, including VRML:

```
http://WWW.Stars.com/Vlib/Providers/VR.html
```

That's it for now. Hopefully, we've given you the information you need to get familiar with VRML, or maybe even to start some VRML implementation on your own. Whatever your objectives, we hope you achieve them!

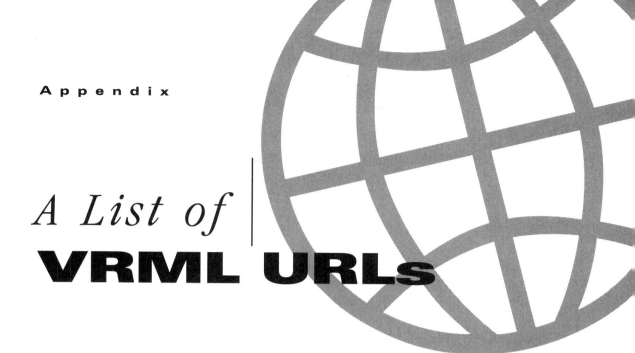

A List of VRML URLs

Chapter 1: The Motivation for VRML

VRML 1.10.3 specification:

```
http://vrml.wired.com/vrml.tech/vrml10-3.html
```

NCSA ftp site, home to many VRML tools and example programs:

```
ftp://ftp.ncsa.uiuc.edu
```

Netscape ftp site, home to several VRML tools and discussions:

```
ftp://ftp.mcom.com
```

SGI site, home of the Inventor file format:

```
http://www.sgi.com/Technology/Inventor.html
```

University of Minnesota site, home to the Object Oriented Graphics Language work:

```
http://www.geom.umn.edu/software/geomview/docs/ooglman.html
```

OOGL viewer's table of contents page:

```
http://www.geom.umn.edu/software/geomview/docs/geomview_toc.html
```

WIRED's information on AutoDesk's Cyberspace Description Format:

```
http://vrml.wired.com/proposals/cdf/cdf.html
```

Information on Roehl's and Bonin's work on a file format for Virtual Worlds (AFF):

```
http://sunee.uwaterloo.ca/~broehl/avril.html
```

Information on Immersive Systems' work on MEME, a virtual world toolset:

```
http://remarque.berkeley.edu/~marc/home.html
```

The Labyrinth Group's seminal paper that led to specification of VRML:

```
http://vrml.wired.com/concepts/pesce-www.html
```

Information about the University of Manchester's Scene Description Language:

```
ftp://ftp.mcc.ac.uk/pub/cgu/MSDL
```

Home page for Virtual Vegas, a gaming and entertainment site with significant VRML capabilities (covered in detail in Chapter 8):

```
http://www.virtualvegas.com/
```

Chapter 2:
Inside VRML: Structure, Syntax, and Concepts

none included

Chapter 3: Advanced VRML: The Saga Continues

Current specification for VRML (version 1.10.3):

```
http://vrml.wired.com/vrml.tech/vrml10-3.html
```

Chapter 4: X Window System Viewers

OpenGL FAQ:

```
http://www.cis.ohio-
state.edu/hypertext/faq/bngusenet/comp/graphics/opengl/top.html
```

These three sites provide information from academia and industry about OpenGL and VRML; all are worth at least a cursory visit:

```
http://hertz.eng.ohio-state.edu/~hts/opengl/article.html
http://www.sgi.com/Technology/openGL/
http://www.sd.tgs.com/~template/Products/opengl.html
```

ftp site that contains background, specifications, and source code for the Graphics Library Utility Toolkit (GLUT):

```
ftp://sgigate.sgi.com/pub/opengl/xjournal/GLUT
```

More information on GLUT, in Web-readable form:

```
http://www.sgi.com/Technology/openGL/glut.html
```

FAQ on SGI Open Inventor format and specification:

```
http://www.sgi.com/Technology/Inventor/FAQ.html
```

Mesa source code and documentation (a freeware implementation of a subset of Open Inventor for non-SGI platforms):

```
ftp://iris.ssec.wisc.edu/pub/Mesa/Mesa-1.2.1.tar.Z
```

Starting point for locating VRWeb for X at the University of Graz:

```
http://hgiicm.tu-graz.ac.at/
```

Information and binaries for SGI's WebSpace VRML viewer for X Windows; the ftp site provides the code's readme file:

```
http://www.sgi.com/Products/WebFORCE/WebSpace/
ftp://sgigate.sgi.com/pub/Surf/WebSpace/tgs/Sun/Readme.txt
```

Information about WebSpace for X, the Template Graphics implementation of WebSpace for non-SGI environments:

```
http://www.sd.tgs.com/~template/WebSpace/monday.html
```

A bogus URL example of the syntax for calling the WebView program with a URL argument:

```
http://vrml.abc.com/vrml_files/house_part1.wrl
```

Chapter 5: VRML on the Mac

Apple's QuickDraw 3D code and information:

```
http://www.info.apple.com/qd3d/QD3D.HTML
```

Source for VRML scene files suitable for use with Whurlwind:

```
ftp://ftp.vrml.org/
```

Download source for the Whurlwind Macintosh VRML viewer:

```
http://www.info.apple.com/qd3d/Viewer.HTML
```

181

Chapter 6: The VRML Windows Browsers

Surveys of Web users, shower proportion of users by platform (Windows Rules!):

```
http://www.netsurf.com/surveys.html
```

Information about Hyper-G and the VRWeb VRML viewer from the University of Graz:

```
http://www.iicm.tu-graz.ac.at/
```

Information about the GopherVR VRML viewer from the University of Minnesota:

```
gopher://boombox.micro.umn.edu
```

Access to the binaries for VRWeb for Windows (may be inactive by the time you read this):

```
ftp://fiicm1pc46.tu-graz.ac.at/ftp/vrshots
```

Source for the Win32s subsystem that lets 32-bit code be used in a 16-bit environment like Windows 3.1, 3.11, or Windows for Workgroups:

```
ftp://ftp.outer.net/pub/mswindows/win32s.zip
```

SGI's WebSpace home page (does not have Windows implementations):

```
http://www.sgi.com/Products/WebFORCE/WebSpace/
```

Template Graphics home page (does have Windows implementation info):

```
http://www.sd.tgs.com/~template/WebSpace/monday.html
```

ftp site for Template Graphics' Windows NT implementation of WebSpace:

```
ftp://ftp.sd.tgs.com/pub/template/WebSpace/WinNT/WS32N10B.EXE
```

Standard DLLs for the Visual C++ runtime libraries, MFC, and OLE:

```
ftp://ftp.sd.tgs.com/pub/template/WebSpace/WinNT/WIN32-DLL.EXE
```

0.8 Alpha 1 version of WorldView for Windows:

```
http://www.webmaster.com/vrml
```

Home page for Infinite Light, the company that distributes the commercial version of WorldView for Windows:

```
http://www.vrml.com/index.html
```

Chapter 7: Post-Modern VRML

Hypertext Hotel MOO:

```
telnet://duke.cs.brown.edu:8888/
```

ChibaMOO (obviously strongly inspired by William Gibson's CyperPunk writings):

```
http://www.sensemedia.net/sprawl/11
```

Home site for WAXweb:

```
http://bug.village.virginia.edu/
```

Chapter 8: The Virtual Vegas Online VRML Site

Virutal Vegas home page:

```
http://www.virtualvegas.com
```

Entry point for would-be participants in VV's Ms. Metaverse Contest:

```
http://www.virtualvegas.com/mm/mmhome.html
```

VV VRML home page (available with VRML viewers only):

```
http://www.virtualvegas.com/vrml/vrml.html
```

Model of VV logo, viewable only for users of SGI's WebSpace:

```
http://www.virtualvegas.com/vrml/vv.wrl
```

Information about the Alias Research Alias Studio 3-D modeling software:

```
http://www.alias.com
```

VV logo, viewable with any VRML viewer:

```
http://www.virtualvegas.com/vrml/vvlink2.wrl
```

VRML scene for VV's Virtual Slot Machine:

```
http://www.virtualvegas.com/vrml/slot.wrl
```

Chapter 9: Virtually There...

Arc home page:

```
http://www.arc.org/vrml/index.html
```

Arc Gallery for the 1995 home page:

```
http://www.arc.org/gallery95/
```

Members of the Arc Gallery jury for 1995:

```
http://www.arc.org/who/jury95.html
```

Chapter 10: The Future of VRML

Cosmological and relativistic VRML models at NCSA:

```
http://jean-luc.ncsa.uiuc.edu/Viz/VRML/
http://www.ncsa.uiuc.edu/General/VRML/
```

Information about BEsoft's development of embedded behaviors within SGI Open Inventor files:

```
http://www.besoft.com/bef/index.html
```

Information about VREAM, Inc.'s Web Interactive Reality Layer interactive Web browser:

```
http://www.vream.com/wirl/
```

Information about the VRML+ development efforts:

```
http://www.worlds.net/products/vrmlplus/index.html
```

Information on Marilyn, a high-performance VR-oriented Web server, and about Tenet, the company that's building this environment:

```
http://www.tenet.net/html/projects.html
```

Information about Virtus Corp.'s Virtus WalkThrough Pro and Virtus VR products, designed to support interactive Web-based VRML walkthroughs:

```
http://www.virtus.com/pr.vrml.html
```

Microsoft's RenderMorphics Reality Lab software does nice things for 3-D visualization in the Windows environment:

```
http://www.gold.net/oneday/render/index.html
```

Hypermail Archive for the VRML mailing list:

```
http://gopher.wired.com/arch/
```

A statement of the goals for the VRML mailing list:

```
http://boris.qub.ac.uk/vrml/concepts/listgoals.html
```

C++ VRML library, QvLib 1.0b1:

```
http://www.eit.com/vrml/qv.html
```

VRML FAQ, a useful source of information that's updated regularly:

`http://www.oki.com/vrml/VRML_FAQ.html`

"Celebrity biographies" of movers and shakers within the VRML community:

`http://boris.qub.ac.uk/vrml/bios/`

Information about Mecklermedia's VR World 95 Convention:

`http://www.mecklerweb.com/shows/vrw95/update.htm`

A VRML authenticator service (to test correctness and conformance to the specification):

`http://www.geom.umn.edu/~daeron/docs/vrml.html`

A VRML Test page:

`http://www-dsed.llnl.gov/documents/tests/vrml.html`

Layne Thomas' "Home World" features an interesting concept and a good *text2wrl* conversion utility:

`http://cs.uah.edu/~lthomas/vrml/`

A nice set of VRML meta-meta pointers:

`http://www.vrml.org/`

A mega-site of VRML references, sites, and tools:

`http://www.lightside.com/3dsite/cgi/VRML-index.html`

Yahoo's VRML search results:

`http://www.yahoo.com/Entertainment/Virtual_Reality/`
`Virtual_Reality_Modeling_Language__VRML_/`

San Diego Center for Supercomputing's VRML repository:

`http://www.sdsc.edu/vrml`

Details on joining a VRML-oriented mailing list:

`http://vrml.wired.com`

Two great general sources of information about Virtual Reality:

`http://www.cs.vu.nl:80/~lgonggr/VRLinks.html`
`ftp://ftp.u.washington.edu/public/virtual-worlds/WWW/scivw-faq.html`

The Virtual Library is a great source for Web programming information of all kinds, including VRML:

`http://WWW.Stars.com/Vlib/Providers/VR.html`

Glossary

.gz. An abbreviation for GNU zip, a (primarily UNIX-based) file compression technique; this is a common file extension for files compressed using this technique.

.tar. An abbreviation for tape archival, *tar* is the eponymous UNIX compression command that creates ".tar"-formatted files. *untar* is the term used to name the operation of decompressing a *tar*red file, even though you'd use the command *tar -xvf junk.tar* to decompress the file named "junk.tar".

.wrl. The file extension required by the VRML specification for so-called "world files," the files that describe VRML scenes. We recommend you include this extension in your MIME-types definitions, so that your VRML browsers will know what to do with such files.

.vrml. A nonstandard, but commonly-used, file extension for VRML "world files," the files that describe VRML scenes. We recommend you include this extension in your MIME-types definitions, so that your VRML browsers will know what to do with such files.

.Z. A format designator associated with the UNIX *compress* program. Use the UNIX *uncompress* program to decompress .Z-formatted files.

abstract. A brief restatement of the contents of a file or document.

AFF ("A File Format For the Interchange of Virtual Worlds"). A file format that consists of tags that possess specific properties, and end up composing a 3-D virtual world (e.g., a material, shape, or texture map). AFF is another precursor to VRML, covered in Chapter 1.

algorithm. A step-by-step, programmatic "recipe" for producing a certain set of results in a computer program.

alias. A computer system name that points at another name, instead of to an underlying object. Most Web URLs are either wholly or partly aliases (to protect the underlying file system on the Web server they point at).

alpha. A way of rating the completion status of a piece of software, alpha indicates that it's still in internal test, and has not yet been released outside its development organization (except under special circumstances, like this book).

anchor. An HTML term for the destination end of a link; it may sometimes be used as a synonym for hypertext links of all kinds.

animation. The use of computer graphics to prepare moving sequences of images; or, any graphic method where the illusion of motion is created by rapid viewing of individual frames in sequence (at least 16 frames per second, usually 30).

ANSI (American National Standards Institute). One of the primary standards-setting bodies for computer technology in the United States.

API (Application Programming Interface). Usually, a set of interface subroutines or library calls that define the methods for programs to access external services (i.e., to somebody else's system or program).

application-independent. A format or facility is said to be application-independent when it works in multiple environments, and doesn't depend on a specific application to understand or use its contents.

archie. A program that catalogs files on over a thousand *anonymous ftp* servers worldwide and lets users search against this database using interactive queries, e-mail, or through other programs like *gopher* or a Web browser.

architecture. The design of a software or hardware system as a connected set of logical building blocks, with sufficient detail to allow each block to be completely designed and implemented, and to allow blocks that interact to successfully communicate with one another.

ASCII (American Standard Code for Information Interchange). A standard encoding for text and control characters in binary format (widely used on most computers).

asynchronous. Literally, "not at the same time," the term refers to computer communications where sender and receiver do not communicate directly with one another, but rather through accessing a common pick-up/drop-off point for information.

attribute. In most object-oriented programming languages, including VRML, an attribute is a named component of an object or term, with specific value typing, element definitions, and requirements and default status.

authentication. A method for identifying a user prior to granting permission to access, change, or delete a system or network resource. It usually depends on a password or some other method of proving that "User A" really is "User A."

authoring tools or **systems**. Software that generates formal code (like VRML) based on how an author manipulates the tool's or system's interface. Because this is much easier than writing VRML by hand, we expect that most VRML development will occur within authoring systems.

back end. Computer science jargon for a service that runs on a machine elsewhere on the network, usually driven by an interface or query facility from another machine elsewhere on the network (the front end).

behavior. A programmatic way of establishing how an object or node "acts" within a virtual reality, behavior describes characteristics that determine motion, response, or action in response to other actors or objects.

beta. A way of rating the completion status of a piece of software, beta indicates that it's been released outside its development organization, but only to a hand-picked group of testers who will use it to try to catch (and let the developers fix) remaining bugs prior to commercial release.

binary. Literally, this means that a file is formatted as a collection of ones and zeros; actually, this means that a file is formatted to be intelligible only to a certain application, or that it is itself an executable file.

binary executables. Files created by compiling (and/or linking) source code modules to create executable files.

BIND (Berkeley Internet Name Domain). BIND is the most popular implementation of the Internet Domain Name Service in use today. Written by Kevin Dunlap for 4.3BSD UNIX, BIND supplies a distributed database capability that lets multiple DNS servers cooperate to resolve Internet names into correct IP addresses.

bitmap. A two-dimensional map of binary digits (bits), destined for use in a one-to-one mapping with a display device's pixels.

boot. As a verb, boot means to start up a computer from its turn-off state. As an adjective (e.g., boot-time) it refers to the computer while it's in the startup phase.

bottleneck. A point in a computer or a network where things become congested and slow down.

boundary errors. In programming, errors can occur within the range of the expected data, outside that range, or right on the edges of the expected range. When errors occur at the edges, they're called boundary errors (e.g., if a number between 1 and 100 is acceptable, what happens with 1 or 100?).

bounding box. For VRML, a bounding box defines the minimum rectangular volume that can contain a node. It defines a "region of operation" that can help to limit the range and complexity of calculations for rendering purposes.

breakpoints. A marked location in a program, usually set with a debugger or an equivalent tool, where the program will halt execution so that the programmer can examine the values of its variables, parameters, settings, etc.

browser. Common usage for a term that describes an application that lets users access WWW servers to surf the Net or view local files. However, other environments like SGML also use browser programs to render markup into viewable information on-screen. In this book, we use the term to match common usage.

BSDI (Berkeley Software Distribution, Inc.). BDSI remains one of the major flavors of UNIX available today, except that now it's distributed by a spin-off business and not the University of California at Berkeley.

bug. An error, problem, or "unsolved mystery" in a computer program.

C. A programming language created by two of the developers of UNIX, Brian Kernighan and Dennis Ritchie.

C++. A programming language developed by Bjarne Stroustrup, C++ is a successor to the C language mentioned above. It is an object-oriented (OO) implementation of C.

CAD (Computer-Aided Design). A computer system designed for creation, engineering, and testing of models and objects.

camera. A VRML node that defines the point of view for a scene graph.

Cartesian projection. A method for organizing breadth, height, and depth in a three-axis graph, where the axes are known as x, y, and z, respectively (developed by the French mathematician, Renee Descartes).

case sensitive. Means that upper- and lowercase letters are not equivalent (e.g., UNIX filenames are case sensitive;"TEXT.TXT" is not the same as "text.txt").

CD-ROM (Compact Disk-Read-Only Memory). A read-only computer medium that looks just like a music compact disk, but contains computer data instead of music.

CGI (Common Gateway Interface). The parameter passing and invocation technique used to let Web clients pass input to Web servers (and on to specific programs written to the CGI specification).

child. In general OO terminology a child is an object contained within another object; in VRML, this means a child node is contained within another (group) node.

class. An object-oriented programming term, class refers to a method for defining a set of related objects that can inherit or share certain characteristics.

clickable image. A graphic in an HTML document that has been associated to a pixel-mapping CGI on the server; users can click on locations of the graphic and thereby retrieve an associated URL.

client pull. A Netscape method where a Web client can instruct a server to send it a particular set of data (e.g., client-initiated data transfer).

client/server. A computing paradigm wherein processing is divided between a graphical front-end application running on a user's desktop machine, and a back-end server that performs data- or storage-intensive processing tasks in response to client service requests.

client. Used as (a) a synonym for Web browser (i.e., Web client), or (b) as a requesting, front-end member for client/server applications (like WWW).

close. A formal communications term that refers to session teardown and termination, usually at the end of a networked information transaction.

compiler. A software program that reads the source code for a programming language and creates a binary executable version of that code.

compliant. Conforms to a defined standard of some kind.

connection. A link opened between two computers for the purposes of some specific communication.

content. The hard, usable information contained in a document.

Content-Type. The MIME designation for file types to be transported by electronic mail and HTTP.

data content model. In SGML, the occurrence notation that describes what other markup is legal within the context of a specific markup element.

DBMS (DataBase Management System). A complex system of programs and utilities used to define, maintain, and manage access to large collections of online data.

debugger. A programming tool used to control the execution of programs under development so that they can be halted and queried at any point during execution.

delimiter. A special text character that indicates a record or field boundary within a text stream, rather than being interpreted as an actual part of the text itself.

development environment. The collection of tools, compilers, debuggers, and source code management resources used as part of the software development process.

Digital Actor. A way of referring to placement of a user within a virtual reality, represented as some kind of virtual object (whether realistic or otherwise).

directory structure. The hierarchical organization of files in a directory tree.

DNS (Domain Name Service). An Internet service that maps symbolic names to IP addresses, by distributing queries among the available pool of DNS servers.

document annotation. The process of attaching comments, instructions, or additional information to a document (usually with annotation software for electronic copy).

document root. The base of a Web server's document tree, the root defines the scope of all the documents that Web users may access (i.e., access is allowed to the root and all its children, but not to any of the root's peers or parents).

document tree. A description of the collection of all directories underneath the document root, with all the documents that each such directory contains.

e-mail (electronic mail). The service that lets users exchange messages across a network; the major e-mail technology in use on the Internet is based on SMTP (Simple Mail Transfer Protocol).

editor. A program used to edit a file; editors are available for specific programming languages, markup languages, and text formats.

element. A basic unit of text or markup within a descriptive markup language.

element type. The kind of value that an element can take (e.g., text, number, and tag).

encoding. A technique for expressing values according to a particular notation (e.g., binary, ASCII, and EBCDIC).

environment variables. Like other UNIX programs CGIs obtain and store their input rather than reading it in every time it's needed. This stored information—in the form of environment variables—is passed to the program by the HTTP server (from the submitting client). An environment variable, therefore, is a value passed into a program or script by the runtime environment on the system where it's running.

error checking. The process of examining input data to make sure it is both appropriate (within specified value or scalar ranges) and accurate (correctly reflects the input).

exception handling. If a program behaves abnormally, encounters an unexpected input, or detects an anomaly in its operation, it must react to such an event. This is called exception handling.

extensibility. A measure of how easy it is to write applications that build upon core mechanisms while adding functionality, new methods, or subclasses (depending on the paradigm).

extension language. A programming language, like Python, that can be used to extend the functionality of programmable languages or interfaces.

FAQ (Frequently Asked Questions). A list of common questions with their answers, maintained by most special interest groups on the Internet, as a way of lowering the frequency of basic technical questions.

field. In a database, a named component of a record and its associated values; in an HTML form, a named input widget or text area and its associated value.

file mapping. A method of supplying a filename to the outside world that does not reveal the complete internal file structures involved (see also alias).

filtering. The process of removing certain objects from a document. For example, removing processing instructions important to a specific scheme not used in a general markup scheme eliminates unintelligible materials.

front end. The user interface side of a client/server application, the front end is what users see and interact with.

ftp (File Transfer Protocol). An Internet protocol and service that provides network file transfer between any two network nodes for which a user has file access rights (especially a remote host and your local host or desktop machine).

gif (also GIF, Graphics Interchange Format). A compressed graphics file format patented by Unisys, and widely used in HTML documents for in-line graphical elements.

GPL (GNU General Public License). A scheme for the mandatory distribution of source code with software devised by Richard Stallman of the Free Software Foundation. GNU tools are incredibly popular with the development community because source code is always available.

grab and twist. The descriptive name for an interactive manipulation technique used in virtual reality interfaces, usually with a data glove, to manage user interaction.

group. Special VRML terminology that describes a node that contains one or more other (child) nodes.

GUI. (Graphical User Interface) A generic name for any computer interface that uses graphics, windows, and a pointing device (like a mouse or trackball) instead of a purely character-mode interface. Windows, MacOS, and X11 are all examples of GUI interfaces.

gzip (GNU zip). The name of the program that produces ".gz" compressed file formats, primarily used in the UNIX world.

helper applications. Applications invoked outside a Web browser to render, display, or play back data that the browser itself cannot handle (e.g., video or multimedia files).

hierarchical. A form of document or file structure, also known as a tree structure, where all elements except the root have parents, and all elements may or may not have children.

HTML (HyperText Markup Language). The text-based descriptive hypertext markup language derived from SGML used to describe documents for use on the WWW.

HTTP (HyperText Transfer Protocol). The TCP/IP-based communications protocol developed for use by WWW, HTTP defines how clients and servers communicate over the Web.

httpd (HTTP daemon). The daemon (or listener) program that runs on a Web server, listening for and ready to respond to requests for Web documents or CGI-based services.

hypermedia. Any of the methods of computer-based information delivery, including text, graphics, video, animation, and sound that can be interlinked and treated as a single collection of information.

hypertext. A method of organizing text, graphics, and other kinds of data for computer use that lets individual data elements point to one another; a nonlinear method of organizing information, especially text.

IICM (Institute for Information Processing and Computer Supported New Media). Graz University's team of talented graphics and Internet programming wizards (part of the team that built the VRWeb VRML viewer).

inheritance. The OO term that indicates that objects subordinate to parent objects or classes obtain attributes or properties from superordinate objects (they "inherit" them from elements higher in the object hierarchy).

instance. A particular incarnation of an object, class, or record, an instance includes the data for one single specific item in a data collection.

interface. The particular subroutines, parameter passing mechanisms, and data that define the way in which two systems (which may be on the same or different machines) communicate with one another.

international standard. In generic terms, an international standard is one that is honored by more than one country; in practice, this usually refers to a standard controlled or honored by the International Standards Organization (ISO).

Internet. The name for a worldwide, TCP/IP-based networked computing community with millions of users worldwide that links government, business, research, industry, and education together.

interpreter. A software program that reads source code from a programming language every time it is run, to interpret the instruction it contains. The alternative is to use a compiler, which translates source code into a binary form only once and which is executed thereafter instead.

IP (Internet Protocol). The primary network layer protocol for the TCP/IP protocol suite, IP is probably the most widely-used network protocol in the world.

ISP (Internet Service Provider). Any organization that will provide Internet access to a consumer, usually for a fee.

jpeg (also JPEG, Joint Photographic Experts Group). A highly-compressible graphics format, designed to handle computer images of high-resolution photographs as efficiently as possible.

keyword. An essential or definitive term that can be used for indexing data, for later search and retrieval; in programming languages, this term is sometimes used to describe a word that is part of the language itself (see also reserved word).

kludge. A programming term for a workaround or an inelegant solution to a problem.

LAN (Local-Area Network). A network linked together by physical cables or short-haul connections, with a span that is generally less than one mile.

library. A collection of programs or code modules that programmers can link to their own code to provide standard, predefined functionality.

link. A basic element of hypertext, a link provides a method for jumping from one point in a document to another point in the same document, or another document altogether.

Lisp (LISt Processing language). A type of programming language for which all operations are defined through the evaluation of a list of functions.

Mac/OS. An abbreviation for the Macintosh Operating System, currently version 7.5.

mail server. Any member of a class of Internet programs (e.g., *major-domo, listserv,* and *mailserv*) that allows users to participate in ongoing data exchanges or file retrieval via electronic mail.

mailing list. The list of participants who exchange electronic mail messages regularly, usually focused on a particular topic or concern.

material binding. In VRML, this refers to the process of associating a material with a node to indicate its composition or other properties.

markup. A special form of text embedded in a document that describes elements of document structure, layout, presentation, or delivery.

Meme (Multitasking Extensible Messaging Environment). An interactive development package from Immersive Systems, Inc. that allows programmers to create virtual worlds and act within them

Mesa. A generic X Window System-based graphics library that supports most of OpenGL's and Open Inventor's implementation aspects and capabilities.

metalanguage. A formal language like SGML that is used to describe other languages.

MIME (Multipurpose Internet Mail Extensions). Extensions to the RFC822 mail message format to permit more complex data and file types than plain text. Today, MIME types include sound, video, graphics, PostScript, and HTML, among others.

mirrored servers. Heavily-used file archives, Web servers, or other network servers may be copied in toto and located around a network, to lower the demand on any one such server and to reduce long distance network traffic. Whenever one server acts as a full copy of another, the second server is said to be a *mirror* of the first.

mirrored site (see mirrored servers).

modularity. The concept that a program should be broken into components, each of which supplies a particular function or capability.

MOO (or MUD, Object-Oriented). A programmable, extensible version of a MUD, in effect a multi-user, text-based virtual reality.

Motif. A UNIX-based GUI.

MUD (Multi-User Dungeon). An Internet-based role-playing game, like *Dungeons and Dragons*, where users gather electronically and interact through typed-in text.

multithreaded. A computer run-time environment that uses a lightweight process control mechanism, called *threading*, to switch contexts among multiple tasks. Whereas a full-context switch may require 150 or more instructions in some operating systems, a thread switch can occur in as little as 30 instructions on some operating systems.

MUSH (Multi-User Shared Hallucination). A "Textual Reality" zone where you can chat with other inhabitants and visit rooms they've created. (Unlike MUDs or MOOs, MUSHes persist in the same "layout" between visits and sessions; they maintain an ongoing, consistent virtual reality.)

NCSA (National Center for Supercomputing Applications). An arm of the University of Illinois where the Mosaic browser was originally developed.

net-pointers. URLs, *ftp* addresses, or other locations on the Internet where you can go to get the "good stuff."

network services. Access to shared files, printers, data, or other applications (e.g., e-mail and scheduling) across a network.

network utilization. The amount of network usage, usually expressed as the percentage of bandwidth consumed on the medium, for a specific period of time (peak utilization of 80% is no big deal; sustained utilization of 80% usually means it's time to divide and grow your network).

newsgroups. Individual topic areas on USENET. Such groups exchange regular message traffic and are a great source of information for technical topics of all kinds.

node. The term for a VRML object, each VRML node defines a "tool" that can be used to help create a 3-D virtual world. A node may be a specific geometric shape (e.g., a sphere or a cube), a texture, or even a movement.

normal. A common technique for calculating the effects of light sources on a scene based on vectors that run perpendicular to the surface of an object; used to estimate the light reflecting off a surface back at the viewer.

NULL. The representation for a missing or empty value.

object-oriented. A programming paradigm that concentrates on defining data objects and the methods that may be applied to them.

OO (abbreviation for object-oriented; see object-oriented).

OpenGL (Open Graphics Language). An industry-standard graphics language administered by the Architecture Review Board, OpenGL defines a rich syntax and structure for 3-D graphics that informs much of VRML (see Chapter 4 for URLs that can provide more information).

Open Inventor. A 3-D graphics description technology created by SGI that helped shape much of VRML and its capabilities as a language (see OIF for more details on its capabilities).

OIF (Open Inventor File format). An ASCII-based file format that supports all of the graphical elements and operations specified in the initial VRML requirements document, including everything from lighting effects to ambient properties.

padding. Additional null values added to the end of a data or byte stream, usually to make sure it consists of an even (or some other specified minimum) number of bytes.

parameter. A value passed into or out of a program, subroutine, or across an interface, whenever code components communicate with one another.

parent. An OO term indicating that an object contains, or is superordinate to another, by inheritance or outright inclusion.

parse tree. A graphical representation of the designation of, and relationships between, tokens or lexical elements in an input stream after that stream has been parsed.

pattern matching. A computerized search operation whereby input values are treated as patterns, and matches are sought in a search database. Whenever exact matches occur, this is called a *hit*; the results of a search produce a list of hits for further investigation.

Perl (Practical Extraction and Report Language). An interpreted programming language developed by Larry Wall, Perl offers superb string-handling and pattern-matching capabilities and is a favorite among Web programmers for CGI use.

pixel (PICture Element). A single addressable location on a computer display, a pixel is the most primitive individual element for controlling graphics (it's also how image maps are measured and specified).

placeholder. A parameter is an ideal example of a placeholder, because it is a symbolic representation that will be manipulated by a program, but only when it's running and an initial input value is defined. While the code is being written, all parameters are merely placeholders.

platform independent. Indicates that a program or device will work on any computer, irrespective of make, model, or type.

polygon. A many-sided surface; polygons provide the basic visual units that VRML uses to define surfaces, and to combine them to represent all kinds of visual objects.

port address. The socket identifier that a program or a service seeks to address for a specific type of communications. Most TCP/IP protocols have "well-known port addresses" associated to them (e.g., HTTP's is 80), but system configurations allow other port addresses to be used (which can sometimes be a good idea for security reasons).

port (short for transport, usually used as a verb). In computer jargon, "porting code" refers to the effort involved in taking a program written for one system and altering it to run on another system.

PostScript. A page description language defined by Adobe Systems, PostScript files usually carry the extension ".ps" in the UNIX world, and are a common format for exchanging nicely-formatted print files.

principle of locality. In computer science terms, this idea conveys the notion that it's a good idea to stay in your own data neighborhood whenever possible. It's a way of designing data retrieval programs to access the hard disk or other, slower forms of storage as seldom as possible, by grabbing larger chunks of information and dealing with them as completely as possible before asking the operating system to deliver more.

processor intensive. An application that consumes lots of CPU cycles (i.e., runs for a long time) is said to be processor-intensive. Good examples include heavy graphics rendering like ray-tracing, animation, CAD, and other programs that combine lots of number-crunching with intensive display requirements.

properties. The values of an object's attributes, or the significance of the attributes themselves, endow an object with properties that distinguish it from other objects.

proprietary. Technology that's owned or controlled by a company or organization, and that may or may not be widely used.

protocol suite. A collection of networking protocols that together define a complete set of tools and communications facilities for network access and use (e.g., TCI/IP, OSI, or IPX/SPX).

pull and manipulate. The descriptive name for an interactive manipulation technique used in virtual reality interfaces, usually with a data glove, to manage user interaction.

push and pop. Operations used to manipulate a programming structure called a stack that uses a "Last-In, First-Out" priority order. When adding an element to a stack, it's called a *push*; when removing an element from a stack, it's called a *pop*. This operation explains how the VRML separator manages stateful information for nodes in a scene graph.

query string. The parameters passed to a Web-based search engine, usually using the GET method. (Because search strings are nearly always short, this is quite safe.)

QuickDraw and **QuickDraw 3D**. Apple Computer's built-in two- and three-dimensional graphics packages, included as part of the MacOS.

QuickTime. Apple's video and animation-rendering library, included with the MacOS, but also available for other platforms (e.g., MS Windows).

radian. A measurement of the arc of a circle, defined by the angle of the radii that define the start and end of the arc.

remote location. A site or machine elsewhere on the network, remote location can also refer to a machine that is only intermittently connected to a network (usually via a dial-up connection).

render. To interpret the contents of a document, image, or other file so that it can be displayed or played back on a computer.

replication. The process of duplicating information on multiple servers, usually according to some strict synchronization protocol or scheme, so that a copy can be said to be an exact replica of the original.

repository. A place where data is kept, like a file archive, database server, or document management system.

request. A network message from a client to a server that states the need for a particular item of information or service.

request header. The preamble to a request, the header must identify the requester and provide authentication and formatting information where applicable. This lets the server know where to send a response, whether or not that request should be honored, and what formats it may be allowed to take.

response. A network message from a server to a client that contains a reply to a request for service.

response header. The preamble to a response, the header identifies the sender and the application to which the response should be supplied.

response time. The amount of time that elapses between the transmission of a request for service and the arrival of the corresponding response.

reusability. The degree to which programs, modules, or subroutines have been designed and implemented for multi-function use. The easier it is to take the same code and employ it in a number of applications, the higher that code's degree of reusability.

rotation. A VRML node's motion around a defined axis that indicates its front-facing orientation.

runtime variables. Program input or output values that cannot be assigned until the program is running.

scale. The size of a VRML node relative to the viewing volume, or to other objects on display in a scene graph.

scene graph (or more simply, scene). The hierarchical file that dictates the sequential order in which VRML nodes must be parsed and rendered.

script. A synonym for *program*; programmers usually refer to their work as a script when it is written in an interpreted language (because, like a script, it is read all the way through each time it's run).

search string. The input passed for keyword search and pattern matching in an index to a search engine or database management system.

separator. A VRML programming construct used to isolate the state of one node from another occurring earlier in a scene graph's node order.

server push. A Netscape-designed technique to let a server initiate data transfer, especially useful for time-sensitive data like voice or video, where rapid delivery is crucial for continuity and intelligibility.

server. Software on a computer that allows other computers to contact it via client software. Also, the computer that runs the server software.

signal to noise. The ratio of good information to irrelevant junk in a newsgroup or mailing list.

snail mail. The antithesis of e-mail, snail mail requires envelopes and stamps, and takes a whole lot longer to get there (at least, when the network's up).

source code. The original text files containing instructions in a particular programming language that programmers write when creating software. If you can see the source code, you have a good shot at understanding what a program is and how it works.

specification. A document that describes the requirements, inputs and outputs, and capabilities of a protocol, service, language, or software program (a kind of "blueprint" for a computer system or service of some kind).

standard. A program, system, protocol, or other computer component that has been declared to be standard may be the subject of an official published standard from some standards-setting body, or it may simply have acquired that status through widespread or long-term use. When talking about standards, it's always important to find out if the designation is official or otherwise.

standards aware. Describes software that understands standards and can work within their constraints.

standards compliant. Describes software that rigorously implements all of a standard's requirements and capabilities; it's a lot more work than standards aware.

state. The manner in which a VRML node is affected by nodes that occur earlier in a scene graph's node order. State can be rigorously controlled by the use of VRML separators.

stateless. A stateless protocol needs no information about what's happened in the past (or expected to happen in the future) about communications between sender and receiver. It's the easiest and most efficient kind of network communication to implement.

step-by-step execution. When debugging a program, locating the exact line of code where an error occurs can be essential to detecting and fixing the problem. Debuggers let developers *step through* their code for this very reason.

stepwise refinement. A phrase coined by Edsger Dijkstra to indicate the repeated respecification and analysis of program elements needed to create elegant designs and implementations.

string. A sequence of characters like "Mike" or "Sebastian."

symbolic link. A mechanism whereby one name points to another name in a system, rather than directly to an object. Symbolic names are common for Web servers, document roots, and other system objects.

synchronous. A method of communications wherein all communicating parties interact with one another at the same time.

syntax. The rules for placing and ordering terms, punctuation, and values, when writing statements in a particular language (including programming languages, where the rules tend to be pretty exact).

system administrator. The individual responsible for maintaining a computer system, managing the network, setting up accounts, and installing applications.

tar (Tape ARchival program). A UNIX utility used to compress and uncompress files (files compressed with this program normally have the extension ".tar").

template. An example or pattern for a program or document, that acts as a predefined skeleton that only needs to be filled in to be complete.

texture. In VRML, a texture defines the appearance of the surfaces of objects.

texture binding. The VRML technique for associating the node that defines a particular texture with a node that defines a shape (or a collection of surfaces).

toolset. A collection of software tools useful for performing certain tasks (e.g., CGI input handling or image map creation).

transform. VRML nodes that apply mathematical functions to control the visual orientation or presentation of the nodes that follow them in a scene graph.

translation. A term used in 3-D graphics to describe a transformation on a node that occurs parallel to the coordinate axes, and contains no rotation or scaling. It describes a linear "move" transformation, where a 3-D vector describes the distance the node moves along each of the axes.

tree. A hierarchical structure for organizing data or documents; common examples include file system directories, object hierarchies, and family trees.

troff. A UNIX text formatting program that uses procedural markup.

UNIX. The powerful operating system developed by Brian Kernighan and Dennis Ritchie as a form of recreation at Bell Labs in the late 60s, still running strong today.

URI (Uniform Resource Identifier). Any of a class of objects that identify resources available to the Web; both URLs and URNs are instances of a URI.

URL (Uniform Resource Locator). The primary naming scheme used to identify Web resources, URLs define the protocols to be used, the domain name of the Web server where a resource resides, the port address to be used for communication, and the directory path to access a named Web document or resource.

URL encoding. A method for passing information requests and URL specifications to Web servers from browsers, URL encoding replaces spaces with plus signs, and substitutes hex codes for a range of otherwise irreproducible characters. This method is used to pass document queries (via the GET method) from browser to servers (and on to CGIs).

URN (Uniform Resource Name). A permanent, unchanging name for a Web resource (seldom used in today's Web environment).

USENET. An Internet protocol and service that provides access to a vast array of named *newsgroups*, where users congregate to exchange information and materials related to specific topics or concerns.

USENET hierarchy. The way in which newsgroups are organized is hierarchical. The most interesting collection of newsgroups, from the standpoint of this book is the *comp.infosystems.www* hierarchy.

USPS (United States Postal Service). See snail mail.

vector. A line segment described by two vertices (location coordinates in a Cartesian space), used for display of that line.

version control. An important aspect of a source code or document management system, version control refers to the ability to associate particular versions of documents or programs together (which may be necessary to maintain a production version and a development version).

viewing volume. The bounding box that defines the space being rendered from a VRML scene graph at any moment.

virtual world. An environment created using a virtual reality modeling tool of some kind, within which users operate and perhaps, interact.

VRML (Virtual Reality Modeling Language). VRML is a language for describing multi-participant interactive simulations—virtual worlds networked via the global Internet and hyperlinked with the World Wide Web.

W3 (World Wide Web).

Web sites. Individual Web document collections named by home pages or other unique URLs.

Webification. The act of turning complex electronic documents in some other format into HTML, usually programmatically rather than by hand.

Webify. (The verb form of Webification; see preceding definition).

WebMaster. The individual responsible for managing a specific Web site.

Webspace. The total agglomeration of sites, resources, and documents available through the World Wide Web.

wireframe. A style of rendering a solid model only by its outlines, rather than using shaded or textured surfaces. Because this kind of rendering requires less computation, designers often work in wireframe views during the development process, to speed their work along.

X11. The GUI standard that governs X Windows controlled by the X/Open Corporation (also the owner of the UNIX trademark and design).

X Windows. A windowed graphical user interface governed by X11 that's widely used in the UNIX community.

Yahoo (Yet Another Hierarchical Officious Oracle). A database written and maintained by David Filo and Jerry Yang, who style themselves "self-proclaimed Yahoos." This is an inauspicious introduction to one of the best search engines for the World Wide Web. When we go surfing, we often start from Yahoo!

Index

IDG BOOKS ®

Order Center: **(800) 762-2974** *(8 a.m.–6 p.m., EST, weekdays)*

Quantity	ISBN	Title	Price	Total

Shipping & Handling Charges

	Description	First book	Each additional book	Total
Domestic	Normal	$4.50	$1.50	$
	Two Day Air	$8.50	$2.50	$
	Overnight	$18.00	$3.00	$
International	Surface	$8.00	$8.00	$
	Airmail	$16.00	$16.00	$
	DHL Air	$17.00	$17.00	$

*For large quantities call for shipping & handling charges.
**Prices are subject to change without notice.

Ship to:

Name _____

Company _____

Address _____

City/State/Zip _____

Daytime Phone _____

Payment: □ Check to IDG Books (US Funds Only)

□ VISA   □ MasterCard   □ American Express

Card # _____ Expires _____

Signature _____

Subtotal _____

CA residents add applicable sales tax _____

IN, MA, and MD residents add 5% sales tax _____

IL residents add 6.25% sales tax _____

RI residents add 7% sales tax _____

TX residents add 8.25% sales tax _____

Shipping _____

Total _____

Please send this order form to:
IDG Books Worldwide
7260 Shadeland Station, Suite 100
Indianapolis, IN 46256

Allow up to 3 weeks for delivery.
Thank you!